Seasonal Variations
of the Eskimo

By the same author

A General Theory of Magic (with Henri Hubert)
The Gift
Sociology and Psychology
Primitive Classification (with Émile Durkheim)
Sacrifice: its Nature and Function (with Henri Hubert)

Seasonal Variations of the Eskimo

A Study in Social Morphology

Marcel Mauss
in collaboration with
Henri Beuchat

Translated, with a Foreword, by James J. Fox

Routledge & Kegan Paul
London, Boston and Henley

Published as 'Essai sur les variations saisonnières des sociétés
Eskimos: étude de morphologie sociale', Part VII of
Sociologie et anthropologie
© Presses Universitaires de France 1950
This translation first published in 1979
by Routledge & Kegan Paul Ltd
39 Store Street,
London WC1E 7DD,
Broadway House,
Newtown Road,
Henley-on-Thames,
Oxon RG9 1EN and
9 Park Street,
Boston, Mass. 02108, USA
Set in Compugraphic Times
and printed in Great Britain by
Ebenezer Baylis and Son Ltd
The Trinity Press, Worcester, and London
English translation © Routledge & Kegan Paul Ltd 1979

British Library Cataloguing in Publication Data

Mauss, Marcel
Seasonal variations of the Eskimo.
1. Eskimos – Social life and customs
I. Title   II. Beuchat, Henri
301.31   E99.E7   79-40172

ISBN 0 7100 0205 X

Contents

Translator's Foreword

> Mauss était un philosophe, un théoricien, qui s'était
> tourné vers le concret, qui avait appris que c'est seule-
> ment au contact étroit des données que la sociologie
> peut progresser.   Louis Dumont

I

In a strict sense, this is the eighth[1] in a series of translations
intended to make available to a wider public the more important essays of the school of the *Année sociologique*. In the
early 1950s, Professor E. E. Evans-Pritchard, together with
colleagues and students of the Institute of Social Anthropology at Oxford,[2] conceived of this undertaking in the
conviction that various essays of the *Année sociologique*
represent a valuable portion of the 'theoretical capital' of
modern anthropology. Individually, each of these essays has
unquestionably contributed to the formation of anthropology and, as such, each can be read for historical interest
as well as for a wealth of ideas that has, by no means, been
exhausted. Yet the original intention, as Evans-Pritchard
insisted, was to produce 'not just translations of uncon-
nected essays but of essays which have a close theoretical
relationship, each illustrating in the discussion of a particular topic a common point of view'.[3] Thus, as a whole,
these translations offer a glimpse of the unique – and all too
brief – conjunction of young scholars whom Émile Durkheim

1

gathered together to work on a common intellectual pro-
gramme: the publication of an annual periodical devoted to
nothing less than the systematic review, elaboration and
analysis of the resources of the social sciences.[4]

A significant feature of this series of translations is, however, its focus on the work of Marcel Mauss. This is itself
indicative of the fact that so much of Mauss's life's work was
inextricably linked with the *Année sociologique*, both with
the original series which ran from 1898 to 1913 and with the
new series which Mauss attempted, unsuccessfully, to revive
in 1925. Four of the eight translations that have so far
appeared are of collaborative works by Mauss published in
the *Année sociologique*. These include his essay on *Sacrifice*,
written with Hubert (1899), on *Primitive Classification*
written with Durkheim (1903), on *A General Theory of
Magic* written with Hubert (1904) and on *The Gift* (1925) –
undoubtedly Mauss's best-known essay – which is no less the
result of a collaborative effort than Mauss's other studies,
since it forms part of an investigation that Mauss undertook
with his colleague, Georges Davy.[5]

This present translation, *Seasonal Variations of the
Eskimo: a Study in Social Morphology*, is a further important essay by Mauss, this time written in collaboration with
Henri Beuchat.[6] As its title suggests, it is both a case study
and a theoretical disquisition. As a case study, it is an
attempt to sort out and make intelligible a large, scattered
but reasonably comprehensive body of ethnographic
information on a single culture. As such, the essay is still
regarded by specialists in the field as an 'illuminating' source
on the Eskimo[7] and has even been recommended by Edmund
Leach as a possible 'prototype for what every British social
anthropologist would like to do with the ethnographic data
which fill his notebooks'.[8]

The theoretical implications of the essay are far more
various. Mauss saw the essay as a demonstration of the tenet,
derived from Mill, that a single case study, well-conceived
and well-executed, is sufficient to establish a general social
principle. The principle here concerns the effects of seasonal
variations within society, for which the Eskimo offered 'a
privileged field of study' because of the extreme prominence
of such variations among them. This initial perception of
seasonal variations has since been reconfirmed and docu-

mented by many anthropologists, not just among the Eskimo, but in other societies, on which there is now a considerable literature. Richard B. Lee, for example, in summarizing some of this literature, cites Mauss's 'classic paper' as the first formal description of this phenomenon which remains a topic of continuing research.[9] For Mauss, however, the critical feature was not merely the recognition of this phenomenon but the establishment of a principle. For this reason, the essay is subtitled: 'A Study in Social Morphology'.

II

The plan of the *Année sociologique* was to encompass the social sciences, and its review 'sections' were therefore intended to embody a general outline of sociology. Most of these review sections retained the same rubric throughout the period of *Année*'s publication: (I) 'General Sociology', (II) 'Religious Sociology', (III) 'Moral and Legal Sociology', (IV) 'Criminal Sociology' (in volume 4, retitled to include 'Moral Statistics'), and (V) 'Economic Sociology'. But, in volume 2, the sixth section, which had previously been labelled 'Diverse' items,[10] was reorganized as 'Social Morphology' and provided with an introduction by Durkheim. In this introduction, Durkheim describes the 'science' of social morphology in these rather general terms:[11]

Social life rests on a substratum which is determined in its size as in its form. This includes the mass of individuals who compose the society, the way in which they occupy the land, and the nature and configuration of objects of every sort which affect collective relations . . . The constitution of this substratum affects, directly or indirectly, all social phenomena in the same way that psychological phenomena are, directly or indirectly, related to the state of the brain. These therefore represent a set of problems which are of evident interest to sociology, relate to one and the same object, and ought to belong to the same science. It is this science which we propose to call *social morphology*.

To complicate matters, despite misgivings expressed in his introduction and in the first review of the new section – an eleven-page assessment of Friedrich Ratzel's *Politische Geographie*, Durkheim invited Ratzel to contribute to the *Année*. Ratzel responded to this request, in the following year, with a short essay on 'Land, Society and the State',[12] but the preponderant geographical emphasis in this 'outside' contribution was hardly in keeping with Durkheim's views. And a few years later, Durkheim alluded to it as an instance of an 'electism' that harmed the impression of the *Année* as a whole.[13] Whatever else it may have done, it did not clarify what was meant by the 'science of social morphology'; nor did subsequent sections on social morphology in later volumes of the *Année* contribute to a coherent conception of this intended science. Many of its subsections changed from year to year and were either too general or too varied to give a clear idea of how they were related to one another. The section on social morphology gave the appearance of having been created as an afterthought, put together from various subjects, and left to occupy an odd position within the *Année sociologique* – a situation which Mauss recognized but did not comment upon until some years later.

From the beginning, Mauss assumed a prominent position within the *Année* group and his role became even more crucial after the loss of many of the younger members and the death of Durkheim. Mauss felt a vital obligation to continue the work of his colleagues but, as time went on, he faced the dilemma of developing a common stock of ideas without altering, too radically, the tradition from which they had emerged. In this, he remained consistently loyal to a Durkheimian inheritance which he attempted to transform. His treatment of the subject of social morphology provides an excellent example of this.

To volume 2 of the new series of the *Année sociologique*, which appeared in 1927, Mauss contributed a long article on the 'divisions' of sociology[14] – his first major statement of this kind since the article on 'Sociology' in *La Grande Encyclopédie* which he wrote with Fauconnet in 1901. He begins his discussion with an attempt to justify the arrangement of the new series which preserved the same organization as the previous volumes: 'We are altering nothing in the outline that Durkheim had slowly elaborated.'[15] He admits, however, that one reason for this is that the 'task of renovation' is 'certainly too great for the handful of Durkheim's students who remain'.[16] Yet, having said this, he can be critical of the existing arrangement and he focuses primarily on the category of 'social morphology':[17]

> Social morphology unites various sciences that are ordinarily but unduly separated, poorly defined, and when joined, are still even more poorly arranged as a group, as is the case with demography and anthropogeography . . . Morphology is a part of sociology, virtually its primordial half, and it is also one of its most independent parts . . . Morphological phenomena have an exceptionally marked material aspect which can be quantified and graphically represented (by charts and diagrams). These phenomena are dependent on one another to such a degree that they seem to form a distinct domain within the social domain. Their theory ought to be, in our view, either the first or the last of our categories of data. The first, if one considers the material form of each society as it presents itself in time and space: the number of individuals, the movement and stability of the population, the succession of generations, the circulation of individuals, the limitation of an area, geographical conditions and adaptation to the land – all of these ought to be, from this point of view, the primary object of our studies, both specialized and general. Or, if one studies the geographical distribution and the demography of different social organizations . . . this aspect of morphology ought to come later. In any case, morphology is poorly placed where it stands in the *Année sociologique*.

Mauss reverts to a discussion of social morphology at several junctures in this same article, insisting that such considerations are methodologically essential and reflect the importance of the study of morphology in his own thinking. But this insistence only highlights the essential ambiguity of his position in retaining a framework whose limitations he is so clearly able to point out. As Mauss notes, the concept of social morphology rests on a dichotomy of social phenomena into 'morphology' and 'physiology' – a distinction that Durkheim borrowed from nineteenth-century biology. On this analogy, social morphology is supposedly the study of 'material structures' and social physiology the study of their 'functioning'. Yet even when this 'primary division' is purged of its vitalistic antecedents, it still involves a distinction that should not be too sharply drawn since the notion of 'structure', as Mauss insists, cannot be confined to the study of material structures.[18]

It would be tempting to see in Mauss's discussion of morphology signs of an emergent structuralism or hints of that 'modernity' of mind for which Claude Lévi-Strauss has praised him, but the fact is that despite his qualifications and critical comments, Mauss retained this primary distinction to the end of his teaching career.[19] It was never the cause for a break in the traditions of sociology which he was committed to uphold.

If, however, we take Mauss as seriously as he intended, and realize the special importance that social morphology had for him as sociology's 'primordial half' and 'first category' of inquiry and if, at the same time, we attend less to his choice of general terminology and more to the specific way in which he himself carried out his only study in social morphology, his essay on the *Seasonal Variations of the Eskimo* takes on a special, and indeed a central, significance. The essay can then be recognized for what it is: the first ethnographic attempt to adopt a holistic, ecological approach to the analysis of a society. As Victor Karady – Mauss's most astute commentator – has already indicated, the idea of a 'total' study of society is implicit throughout the argument of the essay and this links it most closely to his celebrated essay, *The Gift*.[20]

III

We know that Mauss spent over two years on the preparation and publication of his essay on the Eskimo. He began his research, in all probability, shortly after the completion of his essay on *A General Theory of Magic* with Hubert. From 1903 to 1905 he devoted his seminars at the École

Pratique des Hautes Études to an 'examination of texts' on the Eskimo[21] and there is no doubt that his aim was to present a comprehensive view of this population. His footnotes and bibliography comprise nearly half of the total text of the essay and his references come to more than two hundred titles in four principal languages – Danish, English, German and French. It is possible also to detect elements of Mauss's eventual argument in his earlier reviews of Boas's monograph on the Eskimo of Baffin Land and Nelson's study of Bering Strait which appeared in volume 7 of the *Année*.[22] But these and other scattered references to the Eskimo give no hint of the presentation of Mauss's general argument and it is this that deserves special consideration.

In his introduction, Mauss is concerned mainly to state his purpose and to distinguish his study from the 'anthropogeography' of Ratzel. Responding to Ratzel's views was of particular importance to the members of the *Année* as a group and Mauss's reply, succinctly stated, is that 'the land factor must be considered in relation to a social context in all its complex totality.'

Chapter 1 sets forth Mauss's basic orientation which is, essentially, ecological. He examines the 'general morphology' of the Eskimo: those invariant features of the society to which a seasonal morphology can later be related. He defines a specific environmental niche – namely, a northern coastal fringe, and he identifies the Eskimo in relation to this niche. The 'settlement' Mauss sees as the territorial unit of a group of assembled families, and he defines this as 'a concentration of houses, a collection of tent sites', with 'grounds for hunting and fishing on land and sea' and an entire 'system of paths, passages and harbours' that connect these grounds. This is not, therefore, an absolute space but a complexly contoured, somewhat permeable but none the less bounded landscape which, Mauss argues, must possess a specific configuration of minimal requirements to allow the Eskimo to pursue their seasonally variable activities. Since the Eskimo live from hunting and fishing, their way of life reflects a 'necessary symbiotic relation among animal species'. Hence their population density, distribution and even the characteristic composition of Eskimo groups – the result of a low birth-rate and high adult male mortality – are related to a delicate balance of environmental factors.

Mauss, however, concludes this chapter with what appears to be a *non sequitur*. He asserts that 'the limitation on Eskimo settlements depends on the way in which the environment acts, not on the individual, but on the group as a whole.' This is a reasonable statement if one interprets it as a further affirmation of the importance of social factors, but it seems curiously illogical if it is interpreted to imply a kind of group selection, since the data that Mauss has marshalled to make his case clearly show how environmental factors operate on groups via individuals. The latter interpretation seems the more warranted in that Mauss adds a footnote in which he attributes a decisive agency to the 'group' in the abstract. 'Moreover', he writes, 'the group intervenes forcibly, as a group, to limit the number of members in its charge'. Such assertions, while they reflect Mauss's theoretical background, do not necessarily hamper the development of his argument and in some cases, as in this one, they appear to be merely appended to it.

In the next chapter, Mauss begins to elaborate his celebrated contrast between the two seasonal morphologies of the Eskimo. This involves a detailed discussion of various forms of dwellings, regional house types and their internal arrangements. This explicit examination of dwellings as the reflection of particular forms of social organization is intended to substantiate a single, major observation. In summer, individual Eskimo families live in tents, dispersed and scattered over an immense area; in winter, these families congregate in concentrated settlements composed of multifamily houses, often linked to one or more communal houses or *kashim*, where collective ceremonies are performed. It is essential for Mauss to show that 'the two seasons present two entirely different appearances' and that these appearances correspond to two distinct social morphologies.

The remarkable feature of Mauss's discussion is its historical, resource-oriented view of regional variation among the Eskimo, which is all the more remarkable given the scattered and uneven literature on which it is based and the time when it was written. In this view, house forms vary according to the different materials available for their construction, just as the patterns of the settlement in which these houses are found vary according to changing resources and their locations. Frequent references to archaeological data underline the importance of time as a factor in any evaluation.[23] But this variation is not without limits and, in fact, Mauss offers a generalization to encompass certain of its features: 'while the internal density of each separate house varies, as we have shown, according to the region, the density of an entire settlement is always as high as subsistence factors permit. The social volume of a settlement – the area actually occupied and exploited by the group – is kept to a minimum.'

At the same time, Mauss makes it very clear that he does not see the twofold seasonal morphology of the Eskimo as merely the product of environmental conditions, for he notes that this dual morphology persists even in those parts of Alaska where 'the group remains in one place and the reasons for its summer dispersion have disappeared.' He goes on, in the following chapter, to discuss the 'causes' of these seasonal variations. He is not, as he states quite explicitly, interested in all such causes, which would be impossible to reconstruct, but rather in those factors in which one can distinguish social from physical causes. He rejects certain simplistic explanations and in their place notes that, by means of its specific technology, 'Eskimo social life becomes a veritable phenomenon of symbiosis that forces the group to live like the animals they hunt. These animals concentrate and disperse according to the seasons . . . This alternation provides the rhythm of concentration and dispersion for the morphological organization of Eskimo society.' But having made this statement, Mauss immediately qualifies it. Although biological and technological factors are extremely important, 'they are insufficient to account for the total phenomenon.' These factors may account for the onset, duration, succession and even the marked opposition of the periods of concentration and dispersion, but Mauss's concern with a total social phenomenon will not allow him to accept these factors as an adequate explanation of the characteristic cultural features of these different periods.

The whole of the next chapter is taken up with an examination of this 'total phenomenon'. The effects of seasonal variations can be seen, according to Mauss, in all aspects of Eskimo life – on systems of classification, naming procedures, ritual prohibitions, ceremonial activities, kinship and family organization, property rights, sexual relations and moral life in general. But on the verge of grossly over-emphasizing the dichotomy between the seasons, Mauss also indicates some of the mutual influences of one season on the other. These final observations effectively conclude Mauss's description of Eskimo life but this description is itself the occasion for observations of a more general nature.

Thus, Mauss's short, seemingly unobtrusive concluding chapter is a dense concatenation of different ideas. He argues (1) that the qualitative differences in the pattern of Eskimo life are related to quantitative differences in its relative intensity; (2) that winter, as a period of intense social interaction, is the time when individuals become conscious of themselves as a group whereas summer is the time when such social bonds slacken; (3) that this alternation in social life, so evident among the Eskimo, is common to many different societies although there exist 'no absolutely necessary biological or technological reasons' for it and (4) that this, therefore, suggests 'a law that is probably of considerable generality', namely (5) that 'social life does not continue at the same level throughout the year; it goes through regular, successive phases of increased and decreased intensity, of activity and repose, of exertion and recuperation.'[24] Mauss links these propositions to two further propositions which he claims his essay has established. The first is that 'the climacteric conditions of Eskimo life can be accounted for only by the contrast between the two phases of the year and the clearness of their opposition'; the second that because social life is dependent on its material substratum, Eskimo societies offer a special 'test case' for 'at the very moment when the form of the group changes, one can observe the simultaneous transformation of religion, law and moral life.' And it is on the establishment of these propositions that Mauss rests his epistemological claim that 'the analysis of one clearly defined case can establish a general law better than the accumulation of facts or endless deduction.'

IV

Mauss's essay, whose argument we have now considered in some detail, is unquestionably both subtle and persuasive, but it is not entirely free of ambiguities and indeed it contains one major contradiction which has given rise to radically different interpretations of its significance. Thus, for example, the first critical review of the essay, published in 1906 by the distinguished Hungarian sociologist, Oscar Jaszi, hailed the work as 'an inductive vindication of historical materialism' for its demonstration of the 'primary importance' of an economic system and a production pattern. For Jaszi, the essay showed that the 'collocation of populations is primarily determined by the economic opportunities of the environment and the state of technology'.[25] Jaszi's view is by no means a unique judgment. More recently Claude Dubar has similarly argued that this study 'is nothing else but a particular confirmation of the essential relation in Marxist theory between infrastructure and superstructures within a particular social formation'.[26] In contrast to these views, the opposite interpretation of this essay has perhaps best been stated by Mary Douglas.[27] For her, *Seasonal Variations . . .*

> is an explicit attack on geographical or technological determinism in interpreting domestic organization. It demands an ecological approach in which the structure of ideas and of society, the mode of gaining a livelihood and the domestic architecture are interpreted as a single interacting whole in which no one element can be said to determine the others.

Of these two interpretations, the latter is substantially more in keeping with what Mauss seems to have intended and it can be confirmed by reference to numerous passages throughout the essay; the former – Jaszi's interpretation in particular – is none the less a valid extrapolation of the implications of certain of Mauss's statements, especially when these statements are viewed, as Jaszi saw them, in connection with some of Durkheim's statements on social morphology. In general terms, it is possible to trace the ambiguities in *Seasonal Variations* to their source in the three principal texts that Mauss cites to bolster his own argument, namely Durkheim's *Division of Labour, Rules of Sociological Method* and *Suicide*. The uncertainties over 'explanatory priorities' in these books has been lucidly analysed by Steven Lukes in his study of Durkheim[28] and need not concern us here. In specific terms, the contradiction in the essay can be posed succinctly: if the alternation of the seasons merely provides the opportunity for a change in morphology and if, as Mauss indicates, summer dispersion persists in areas where the environmental reasons for it have ceased to exist and winter congregation recurs in summer under favourable conditions, then there can be no question of a simple determination of Eskimo social life by its material substratum. If, on the other hand, as Mauss also argues in his concluding paragraph, the Eskimo present a special test case precisely because when the form of the group changes, there is a simultaneous transformation of their social life and this occurs 'every year with absolute invariability', a strict determination, rather than a complex dependency, is clearly attributed to the material substratum of the society.

Neither its various ambiguities, especially on the nature of social morphology, nor the contradiction with which it ends have seriously affected the importance of this essay. Although it still betrays hints of a quest for some kind of simple, unitary explanation of social phenomena, which the whole of Mauss's later work belies, and although it exhibits a tendency to overstructure its analysis to develop its argument, *Seasonal Variations* remains as a remarkable first attempt to develop an ecological approach within which to consider a whole range of complex social phenomena. Its influence has, therefore, been limited neither to a consideration of the details of its argument nor to its case study of the Eskimo.

V

It frequently happens that a particular study has its greatest influence beyond its intended realm of analysis. It is perhaps, therefore, not altogether surprising that *Seasonal Variations* did not have a major influence on the development of Eskimo studies, especially since Beuchat who was chosen to advance these studies died, most tragically, at the very beginning of his fieldwork in the Arctic. On the other hand, as a model of ethnographic description, *Seasonal Variations* has had considerable influence. A clear and unmistakable example of this influence can be seen in Evans-Pritchard's classic study, *The Nuer*, published in 1940. Evans-Pritchard himself left no doubt about his intellectual allegiance to the school of the *Année sociologique*,[29] and his colleague, Godfrey Lienhardt, has already admirably sketched the relations between these two seemingly unrelated ethnographic analyses.[30]

The Nuer, some 400,000 people divided into various tribes, are cattle herders who occupy an area quite unlike that of the Eskimo. Instead of a northern coast fringe, Nuerland is a vast plain in the southern Sudan, intersected by three great rivers whose seasonal flooding sets a pattern for the year. In summer, the rains fall and the rivers rise flooding all of the countryside except for scattered areas of elevated land; in winter, the waters recede to form an immense, increasingly dry savannah. In the wet season, the Nuer must move to high ground to plant their crops and raise their cattle until the rivers subside and they can move out onto the plain where they gradually congregate with their herds in large camps along river banks. This mixed economy which combines horticulture, fishing and cattle husbandry, nevertheless follows a pattern which, as Evans-Pritchard describes it, is like that described by Mauss for the Eskimo. Not merely the model, but the very language which Evans-Pritchard uses, recalls Mauss's essay. In the conclusion to this discussion of Nuer ecology, he writes:[31]

> The oecological rhythm divides the Nuer year into two divisions, the wet season when they live in villages and the dry season when they live in camps, and camp life falls into two parts, the earlier period of small, temporary camps and the later period of large concentrations in sites occupied every year.

As a comparable case study, however, *The Nuer* can hardly be seen to confirm all of Mauss's conclusions. The chief Nuer ceremonies of initiation are not held at the time of maximum concentration but almost invariably at the end of the rainy season when the Nuer are still living in their separate villages and have plenty of food for their festivities. But a consideration of *The Nuer* makes clear the fact that it is, by no means, a piece of naive ethnographic description; it is part of a tradition of ethnographic writing, whose sources are as important to recognize as the social phenomena they report.

In tracing these sources, it is equally important to recognize some of the more prominent influences on Mauss. *Seasonal Variations*, for example, refers to no less than seventeen separate articles or monographs written by ethnographers associated with the Smithsonian Institution or the Bureau of American Ethnology. The work of many of these ethnographers, as Mauss explicitly notes, was closely related to the attempt at ecological analysis in *Seasonal Variations*. In particular, Mauss cites the series of related ethnographic lectures by McGee, Mason, Powell, Hubbard and Fewkes delivered at the United States National Museum in 1896 'with the view of illustrating the relations of life to environment, especially on the American continent'.[32] And behind the stentorian rhetoric of these lectures, one can glimpse some of the ideas that Mauss may have found congenial and which contributed to a common ecological perspective within anthropology.

VI

Mauss wrote of Beuchat, his student and collaborator, that 'he knew a great many things and he knew them well'. Apart from his work with Mauss on *Seasonal Variations*, Beuchat contributed only one other piece to the *Année sociologique*, a short review of Bowditch's book on the Mayan calendar for volume 12 of the *Année*. His main work was his *Manuel d'archéologie américaine*, an 800-page encyclopedic survey of the discovery of the Americas and of the prehistory and development of major Indian cultures, published in Paris in 1912; he also wrote a number of articles with Paul Rivet on the linguistic classification of Indian languages in South

America. Beuchat's chief interests seem to have been in working out connections between populations, their movements and cultural developments. An early interest in the Eskimo and the opportunity to take part in one of the largest and best-equipped scientific explorations of its kind undoubtedly prompted him to join Vilhjálmar Stefánsson's Canadian Arctic expedition of 1913. This expedition, with a scientific staff of fifteen including another anthropologist, Diamond Jenness (who together with Beuchat and Stefánsson was assigned to the study of Eskimo life), set sail in three ships from Nome, Alaska, in July 1913. Of these three ships, the *Karluk*, with the main contingent of the expedition, became locked in ice on 13 August and drifted erratically in a north-westerly direction for several months until, under mounting ice pressure, it broke and sank on the afternoon of 11 January 1914. The members of the expedition faced an enormously complex logistic problem of moving themselves and their supplies in stages from their shipwreck camp on an ice-floe in the Arctic Ocean to Wrangel Island, the closest land in their vicinity. It was during this operation that Beuchat and three other men decided on an attempt to reach land on their own. This meant trekking, via Wrangel Island, to the Siberian mainland. They left the main camp on 5 February, and they were encountered four days later by two members of the expedition who were moving supplies in advance of the main party. Beuchat's hands and feet were severely frozen; he was partly delirious; but he refused to return to the main camp. Thereafter his party was never seen or heard of again and no trace of them was ever found.[33] In Mauss's words: 'In the wreckage, all the notes that Beuchat had begun to take were lost along with the many studies he had brought with him to finish during the long Artic winters.'[34]

VII

Lévi-Strauss has written of the remarkable 'modernity' of Mauss's thought. The evidence of *Seasonal Variations*, I believe, supports this claim and is sufficient justification for the present translation. But this modernity also poses its own problems. So many of Mauss's ideas have borne fruit that there is a temptation to render them in a language and terminology of a later date. This would be a disservice to Mauss, whose ideas at the time were still in a crucial formative phase. Therefore, as translator, I have endeavoured to keep as close to Mauss's own terminology and mode of phrasing as the demands of fluent English allow. In Mauss's writing, one can detect a certain tension – a subtle combination of assertion and qualification – that is as evident in the phrasing of his sentences as in the ordering of his argument. I interpret this as an indication of what Dumont has described as Mauss's chief quality – that of a theoretician with a superb speculative mind who was committed to the concrete analysis of social phenomena.

To appreciate this aspect of Mauss, one must also give close attention to the notes to *Seasonal Variations* which comprise a considerable portion of the essay. In the original, these notes were located at the bottom of each page and were thus perceptibly an integral part of the argument. Unfortunately, however, they were set forth in a style of scholarship that seems to have intended that they be interpreted as memoranda rather than as precise references. Although these notes demonstrate a formidable erudition and greatly enhance an understanding of Mauss's interpretation of his sources, they abound in ambiguities and inaccuracies. A major task in the preparation of this edition has been to establish a reasonably complete and accurate bibliography and to use this bibliography to correct references throughout the notes. Only about five, from more than two hundred references, have proved impossible to trace. In some cases, this has meant reconstructing the way Mauss created nonexistent sources (see n. 3 to the Introduction), how he confused different authors with the same last name (see n. 25 to chapter 1), or how he seems to have conflated similar titles of separate books (see n. 112 to chapter 2).

The notes in this edition are linked to the bibliography. Authors are identified by name and their works by date of publication. I have attempted to identify authors of several books or papers who were referred to, in the original, by name only, according to the work which Mauss seems to have had in mind. I have also tried to locate the exact source of all direct quotations and to provide, in the notes, the original version where there appears to be some discrepancy. On the other hand, the checking of all specific page references in cited works was beyond my capacity and I have left these precisely as they appear in the original. Undoubtedly there remain inaccuracies in certain of these notes and minor inconsistencies in the spelling of some proper names due to the various languages of the original sources, but preparation of this work has already taken far longer than I initially contemplated. Moreover, at this date, the importance of an English translation of *Seasonal Variations* lies primarily in the presentation of Mauss's ideas rather than in the correction of particular aspects of his scholarship.

Here I wish to thank various individuals who have helped me in the preparation of this work: Dr Steven Lukes of Balliol College, Oxford, for supplying me with a personal copy of an obscure article which I might otherwise have been unable to obtain; Henny Fokker-Bakker of the Department of Anthropology, Research School of Pacific Studies, The Australian National University, Canberra, for assistance in the initial phase of my bibliographic searches; and colleagues and staff of the Netherlands Institute for Advanced Study, Wassenaar – where this work was finally completed – in particular, Dinny Young and Simon Andriesen of the Library staff and Marina Voerman who had the task of typing the manuscript. Finally, and above all, I must express special thanks to my wife, Irmgard, who assisted in all stages of the preparation of the notes and bibliography.

Wassenaar   JJF

Introduction[1]

We propose to study here the social morphology of Eskimo societies. By this term, social morphology, we refer to the science whose investigations are intended not just to describe but also to elucidate the material substratum of societies. This includes the form that societies assume in their patterns of residence, the volume and density of their population, the way in which the population is distributed, as well as the entire range of objects that serve as a focus for collective life.[2]

However, since this work deals with a specific geographical population,[3] we want to avoid giving it the appearance of a purely ethnographic study. Our intention is not to collect, in one descriptive monograph, all sorts of diverse facts about Eskimo morphology. On the contrary, we intend to establish certain general relations about the Eskimo. We have chosen this remarkable people as the special object of our study precisely because the relations to which we wish to call attention are exaggerated and amplified among them; because they stand out, we can clearly understand their nature and significance. As a result, it is easier to recognize them even in other societies where they are less immediately apparent or where a configuration of other social facts conceals them from the observer. The Eskimo offer such a privileged field of study because their morphology is not the same throughout the year. The way in which the Eskimo group together, the distribution of their population, the form of their houses and the nature of their settlements all change completely in accordance with the seasons. These variations which, as we shall see, are considerable, offer favourable conditions for a study of how the material form of human groups – the very nature and composition of their substratum – affects different modes of collective activity.

We may perhaps find that only this one population provides the appropriate basis for a study whose aim is to establish propositions that are more widely applicable. But we must not lose sight of the fact that the Eskimo occupy an extensive coastal area.[4] There exist, not one, but many Eskimo societies[5] whose culture is sufficiently homogeneous that they may be usefully compared, and sufficiently diverse that these comparisons may be fruitful. Moreover, it is wrong to assume that the validity of a scientific proposition is directly dependent on the number of cases that can supposedly confirm it. When a relation has been established in one case, even a unique case but one that has been carefully and systematically studied, the result is as valid as any that can be demonstrated by resorting to numerous facts which are but disparate, curious examples confusingly culled from the most heterogeneous societies, races or cultures. John Stuart Mill states that a well-constructed experiment is sufficient to demonstrate a law; it is certainly infinitely more indicative than numerous badly-constructed experiments. Indeed this methodological rule applies just as much to sociology as to the other natural sciences. Hence, at the end of this work, we intend to refer to certain facts which indicate that the relations that we are about to establish for the Eskimo are more generally applicable.

In treating these questions, we should clarify our position in regard to the methods practised by that special discipline known as anthropogeography.[6] The facts that anthropogeography deals with are, in a sense, of the same sort as those with which we are going to be concerned. Anthropogeography also proposes to study the distribution of men on the surface of the earth and the material form of societies; and no one can rightly deny that the research undertaken in this direction has had important results. It is certainly not our intention to belittle the positive discoveries or the fruitful suggestions which we owe to this brilliant array of researchers. In conceiving of societies as groups of men organized at specific points on the globe, we are not going to make the mistake of considering them as if they were independent of their territorial base; clearly the configuration of the land, its mineral riches, its fauna and flora affect the organization of society. However, since the scholars of this school are specialists in geography, they are naturally inclined to see things from a particular angle; hence by the very nature of their studies they have attributed an almost exclusive preponderance to geographical factors.[7] Instead of investigating all aspects of the material substratum of societies, they have concentrated their attention first and foremost on the factor of land. This is the prime consideration in their research; and the main difference between them and ordinary geographers is that they consider land particularly in relation to society.

They have, however, attributed to this factor a kind of perfect efficacy, as if land were capable of producing effects on its own[8] without interacting with other factors that might reinforce or neutralize its effects either partially or entirely. We need only open the works of the most reputable of these anthropogeographers to see this conception translated into chapter headings: a successive discussion of land in relation to habitation, land in relation to the family, land in relation to the state, etc.[9] Land, however, does not produce effects except in conjunction with thousands of other factors from which it is inseparable. The existence of mineral resources is an insufficient condition for determining human residence at a specific point in a region; a certain stage of industrial technology is needed to exploit them. For men to gather together, instead of living in a dispersed fashion, it is insufficient simply to assert that the climate or a configuration of the land draws them together; their moral, legal and religious organization must also allow a concentrated way of life.[10] Although the geographical situation is an essential factor to which we must pay the closest possible attention, it still constitutes only one of the conditions for the material form of human groups. In most cases it produces its effects only by means of numerous social conditions which it initially affects, and which alone account for the result. In short, the land factor must be considered in relation to a social context in all its complex totality. It cannot be treated in isolation.

So, when we study its effects, we must trace their repercussions on all the categories of collective life.[11] All these questions are not, therefore, geographical questions but proper sociological ones; and in this study we will approach them in a sociological spirit. If we prefer to refer to the discipline to which this study belongs as social morphology rather than anthropogeography, this is not because of some frivolous taste for neologisms but because these different labels define a difference in orientation.

Moreover, though the anthropogeography of the Eskimo has frequently attracted geographers, who are for ever curious about the problems posed by the polar regions, the subject with which we are going to be concerned has hardly been dealt with at all in their works, except in an incidental and fragmentary way. The two most recent works on the Eskimo are H. P. Steensby, *Om Eskimo Kulturens Oprindelse*, and F. Riedel, 'Die Polarvölker'.[12] The first, which is the better of the two, is more of an ethnographic study; its primary purpose is to demonstrate the unity of Eskimo culture and to search for its origin; these the author thinks he can find elsewhere than among the Eskimo themselves, though he has little evidence to support his thesis. The other is more exclusively a geographical work; it contains the best description that we have so far of Eskimo tribes and their habitat. But it maintains the theory – in an exaggerated form which is perhaps not surprising in a student dissertation – of the exclusive action of the land factor. Other published works deal almost entirely with the problem of migrations. These include works by Curt Hassert, Franz Boas, Ernst Wächter, G. Isachsen and A. Faustini.[13] The third part of O. T. Mason's work[14] on modes of transport is particularly concerned with the Eskimo, but this study deals mainly with technology, principally that of travel and transport.

In the end, Steensby is practically the only person who has paid some attention to the specific question of the seasonal variation of Eskimo morphology. To deal with it, our only recourse is, therefore, to the direct reports of observers.[15]

1 General Morphology

Before we begin our investigation of the special forms of morphology that Eskimo societies assume at different times of the year, we must first determine their invariant features. Despite the changes in Eskimo morphology, certain fundamental features always remain the same, and upon these depend the particular variables with which we are going to be concerned. The location of these societies and the number, nature and size of their elementary groups constitute immutable factors. The periodic variations which we are going to describe and elucidate are based on this permanent foundation. We must, therefore, first try to understand this foundation. In other words, before considering the seasonal morphology of Eskimo societies, we must determine the essential features of their general morphology.[1]

Eskimo are[2] to be found between 78° 8′ latitude in the north (the Itah settlement at Smith Strait on the north-west coast of Greenland[3]) and 53° 4′ in the south, on the west coast of Hudson Bay, which is the furthest point to which Eskimo regularly travel but not where they reside.[4] On the coast of Labrador, they are found up to 54° latitude and on the Pacific as far north as 56° 44′.[5] The Eskimo thus cover an immense area of 22 degrees of latitude and almost 60 degrees of longitude, extending into Asia, where they have a settlement at East Cape.[6]

In this vast region, however, both in Asia as well as in America, they occupy only the coasts. The Eskimo are essentially a coastal people. Only a few tribes in Alaska

23

inhabit land in the interior.[7] These are the Eskimo who are settled on the Yukon delta and the Kuskokwim, and who may be considered as maritime river-dwellers.

It is possible, however, to be more precise. The Eskimo are not simply a coastal people. They are people of the water's fringe – if we may use this term to designate all the relatively abrupt terminations of the sea coasts. This explains the marked differences between the Eskimo and other arctic peoples.[8] Except for the deltas and the little-known rivers of King William Land, all the coasts that the Eskimo occupy have the same character: a more or less narrow strip of land skirting the edges of a plateau that gives way, more or less abruptly, to the sea. In Greenland, the mountains overhang the sea; and, moreover, the immense glacier which has been given the name *Inlandsis* (Inland Ice) leaves only a mountainous belt whose widest part (wide on account of the fiords) measures a scant 140 miles. This belt is broken by the outlets to the sea made by the inland glaciers. The fiords and the islands in the fiords are the only areas that are protected from the strong winds and, as a consequence, they enjoy a bearable temperature. They alone offer grazing land for game animals, and readily accessible areas where marine animals can catch fish or may themselves be caught.[9] Like Greenland, the Melville Peninsula, Baffin Land and the northern shores of Hudson Bay also have steep, dissected coasts. Even where the interior plateau is free of glaciers, it is swept by winds and always covered by snow; it offers little habitable land except for a narrow margin along the shore, and deep valleys abutting on glacial lakes.[10] Labrador has the same character, but with an interior climate that is more continental.[11] The Saint Lawrence area of northern Canada and the Boothia Peninsula end in a more gentle expanse, especially at Bathurst Inlet, but, as in other regions, the interior plateau restricts to a relative minimum the area which, when seen on a map, appears as if it ought to be habitable.[12] The coast to the west of the Mackenzie River has the same features from the end of the Rocky Mountains as far as the icy headland at Bering Strait. From this point all the way round to Kodiak Island, the southern limit of the Eskimo zone, there is alternately delta tundra and steep-falling mountains or plateaux.[13]

If the Eskimo are a coastal people, the coast is not for them what we ordinarily think of as a coast. Ratzel[14] has defined 'coasts' in a general way as 'the points of communication between the sea and the land or, rather, between this land and other more distant lands'. This definition does not apply to the coasts that the Eskimo inhabit.[15] Between them and the land behind them there is generally very little communication. The peoples of the interior do not spend much time on the coast,[16] nor do the Eskimo move far inland.[17] The coast is here exclusively a habitat; it is neither a passage nor a point of transition.

After this description of the Eskimo habitat, we must consider how the Eskimo are distributed over the land they inhabit: the particular composition of their social groups, their number, size and disposition.

First, we must know something about the political groupings that comprise the Eskimo population. Do the Eskimo form distinct tribal aggregates, or a nation – a confederation of tribes? Unfortunately, besides its lack of precision, the usual terminology is difficult to apply here. Eskimo society is, by its very nature, somewhat vague and fluid and it is not easy to distinguish which fixed units make up its composition.

A distinct language is one of the surest criteria for recognizing a collectivity, either a tribe or a nation. But the Eskimo show a remarkable linguistic unity over a considerable area. Where we do have information on the boundaries between various dialects,[18] which is not often, it is impossible to establish a definite connection between the area of a dialect and a specific social group. Thus, in the north of Alaska, there are two or three dialects spoken by ten or twelve groups which some observers have thought they could distinguish and to which they have applied the term 'tribe'.[19]

Another criterion that distinguishes a tribe is a common name shared by all its members. But, on this point, it is clear that the tribal nomenclature is very imprecise. In Greenland, there is no mention of any name that refers to a properly-defined tribe, or, in other words, to an agglomeration of local settlements or clans.[20] For Labrador, the Moravian missionaries have not recorded a single proper name. The only names that we do have are for the Ungava district on Hudson Strait, and these are extremely vague and hardly proper names at all (they refer to 'distant people', or 'people of the islands', etc.).[21] It is true that in other areas there are more clearly defined lists of names.[22] But with the exception of Baffin Land and the west coast of Hudson Bay, where names appear to have stayed the same and are reported identically by all authors,[23] there are very serious discrepancies everywhere among observers.[24]

A similar vagueness also applies to boundaries. A boundary is still the clearest indication of the unity of a group who think of themselves as a political entity. But there is only one mention of this, and that applies to the least known portions of the Eskimo population.[25] Tribal warfare is yet another way whereby a tribe affirms its existence and identity; but we know of no case of tribal warfare except among the central Eskimo and the Alaskan tribes for whom there exist special circumstances.[26]

From all these facts, we cannot conclude with complete assurance that there is absolutely no tribal organization among the Eskimo.[27] On the contrary, there are a number of social aggregates that definitely appear to have some of the features which ordinarily define a tribe. Yet, at the same time, it is apparent that more often than not these aggregates assume very uncertain and inconsistent forms; it is difficult to know where they begin and where they end. They appear to merge easily and to form multiple combinations among themselves; and rarely do they come together to perform common activities. If therefore the tribe exists, it is certainly not the solid and stable social unit upon which Eskimo groups are based. The tribe, to be more precise, does not constitute a territorial unit. Its main characteristic is the constancy of relations it permits between assembled groups. Among such groups, communications are more easily maintained than if each group seized upon its own territory and identified with it and if fixed boundaries clearly distinguished different groups from their neighbours. Eskimo tribes are separated from one another by barren expanses, completely denuded and hardly habitable, with headlands round which it is impossible to navigate at any time. As a result, journeys between tribes are a rarity.[28] It is indeed remarkable that the only group that gives the impression of being a proper tribe is the group of Eskimo at Smith Strait. Geographical circumstances have completely isolated it from all other groups and, although it occupies an immense area, its members form, as it were, a single family.[29]

The true territorial unit is, rather, the settlement.[30] By this we mean a group of assembled families who are united by special ties and who occupy a habitat in which they are unevenly distributed, as we shall see, at different times of the year, but which constitutes their domain. A settlement is, thus, a concentration of houses, a collection of tent sites, plus hunting-grounds on land and sea, all of which belong to a certain number of individuals. It also includes the system of paths, passages and harbours which these individuals use and where they continually encounter one another.[31] All this forms a unified whole that has all the distinct characteristics of a circumscribed social group.

(1) The settlement has a definite name.[32] Although other tribal or ethnic names may fluctuate and are reported differently by various authors, the names of settlements are clearly localized and are always reported as the same. As good evidence of this, one need only compare the list of Alaskan settlements which we cite later (Appendix 1) with the one compiled by Petroff. Except for the so-called Arctic district, these lists hardly differ at all, whereas the tribal names that Porter cites are very different from those of Petroff.[33]

(2) The name of a settlement is a proper name used by *all* its members and by them alone. Ordinarily, the name consists of a descriptive place name followed by the suffix -*muit* ('native of—'). [34]

(3) The territory of a settlement has clearly recognized boundaries. Each settlement has its grounds for hunting and fishing on land and sea.[35] Tales tell of their existence.[36] In Greenland, Baffin Land and in the north of Labrador, settlements are strictly localized comprising a fiord with its upland grazing lands. Elsewhere they include either an island with the coast facing it, a headland with its hinterland,[37] or the bend of a river in a delta with a bit of coast, etc. Except when a major catastrophe destroys the settlement, the same people or their descendants always stay in the same spot: the

descendants of Frobisher's victims in the sixteenth century still remembered that expedition in the nineteenth century.[38]

(4) The settlement has more than just a name and a territory; it also possesses a linguistic unity as well as a moral and religious one. Although these two categories may appear initially to be unrelated, we have purposely linked them because the linguistic unity to which we wish to call attention has a religious basis and is related to ideas about the dead and their reincarnation. Among the Eskimo, there exists a remarkable system of taboos concerning the names of the dead, and the entire settlement must observe this taboo. It involves the radical suppression of all words contained in the proper names of deceased individuals.[39] It is also a regular practice to give the name of the last person to die to the first child to be born thereafter in the settlement; the child is considered to be the reincarnation of the dead person. Thus, each locality possesses a limited number of proper names which consequently constitute an element of its physiognomy.[40]

In summary, with the single qualification that settlements, to a certain extent, permeate one another, we can say that each of them constitutes a fixed and defined social unit which contrasts with the changing aspect of tribes. We must not, however, exaggerate the importance of our single qualification because, even if it is true that there is some exchange of population between settlements, this relative permeability[41] or mobility is always caused by vitally urgent necessities. As a result, all variation is readily explicable; hence the rule does not seem to be violated.

We have thus shown that the settlement is the unit that provides the basis of Eskimo morphology. But if we want to be more precise in our representation of it, we must investigate the distribution of settlements in a territory, their size, and the composition of their population according to sex, age and status.

Among the Greenland tribes on which we have good information, there are few settlements. In 1821 Graah found only seventeen between Cape Farewell and Graah Island; it is unlikely that he missed any, since his expedition was carried out under reasonably good conditions.[42] Since then, the number of these settlements decreased, and when Holm made his visit in 1884, nearly all had disappeared. Today the area is almost completely deserted.[43] This progressive diminution has two causes. First, since 1825, European settlements in the south have attracted Eskimo from the east to Frederiksdal because of their resources and the greater protection they offered.[44] Second, settlements further north have become centred upon Angmagssalik.[45] It is reasonable to suppose that the retreat of the Eskimo from Scoresby Sound, which preceded the arrival of Scoresby in 1804, may have come about in the same way, but by force in this case, and not simply from self-interest.

These few settlements are also small and widely separated. At Angmagssalik fiord, which comprises a considerable coastal area, there were only fourteen settlements in 1883 with a total of 413 inhabitants. Ikatek, the biggest, had fifty-eight people; the smallest, Nunakitit, had only fourteen.[46] Moreover it is interesting to follow the movements of the population as indicated in Table 1. One can see how precarious and unstable is the existence of this population. In eight years from 1884 to 1892 it lost, either through death or emigration, two-thirds of its able-bodied members. In 1896 the situation was suddenly reversed by a single favourable year and through help provided by the permanent settlement of Europeans: the population rose from 247 to 372, an increase of 50 per cent.

We have very precise and detailed information on the western coast population.[47] But since it dates from the period after the arrival of Europeans, we will use it only to illustrate two particular points that are equally evident at Angmagssalik.[48] The first is the high level of male mortality and, as a consequence, the considerable proportion of women in the total population. In southern Greenland, from 1861 to 1891, 8.3 per cent of deaths were the result of kayak accidents; in other words, these related exclusively to men who capsized in their dangerous little boats. Only 2.3 per cent of deaths were the result of other mishaps. Another remarkable feature is the number of violent deaths. For northern Greenland, the figures are 4.3 per cent for deaths in kayaks and 5.3 for other violent deaths. For Angmagssalik, according to the information of Holm and Ryder, violent deaths among men are

Table 1

Year	Census	Total population	Males	Females	Births	Deaths	Tents	Settlements (houses)	Emigration or immigration
1884[a]	Holm	413	193	220	5	13	37	14(15)	
1892[b]	Ryder	293	132	161	92[g]	107	29	11	−118[h]
1894[c]	Petersen-Ryberg	235	—	—	—	—	—	—	—
1895[d]	Petersen-Ryberg	247	108	139	5	5	—	13	+12
1896[e]	Petersen-Ryberg	372	166	216	14	7	26	14	+118[i]
11897[f]	Petersen-Ryberg	372	161	211	19	19	27	13(14)	+20/−20[j]

a Holm (1888, pp. 193 ff.).

b Ryder (1895a, pp. 163 ff.).

c Ryberg (1898, p. 129, col. 1). The journal by Petersen, an agent of the Royal Company, gives only summary indications for this year, the year of the foundation of the settlement. The considerable fall was mainly because of a terrible flu epidemic that followed the visit by Ryder's expedition; see Holm (1894, pp. 247 ff.; 1895, p. 89).

d Ryberg (1898, p. 129, col. 2) notes that twelve individuals arrived before 31 December 1894 but that they were not counted.

e Petersen in Ryberg (1898). The year 1895-6 was particularly favourable by contrast to 1894-5, as is evident from the few deaths compared to births. For the number of tents, see Ryberg (1898, p. 118).

f Ryberg (1898, p. 170).

g Ryder (1895a, p. 144) attributes the difference between his census and that of Holm to the poor information about births.

h Ryder (1895a) says that the emigration was directed toward the south.

i The 118 emigrants noted by Ryder all came back; during the four years they were away, births and deaths balanced each other out; see Ryberg (1898, p. 119, col. 2).

j Three *umiaks* (women's boats) left and another, with twenty Eskimo, returned.

[No attempt has been made to resolve apparent inconsistencies in these figures. JJF.]

estimated to account for 25 to 30 per cent of the total mortality rate.[49]

The second point we wish to note concerns the migrations that limit the population of each settlement. The tables which Ryberg provides us for the years 1805 to 1890 demonstrate this fact for the northern districts of southern Greenland. The settlements of Godthaab and Holstenborg increase steadily to the detriment of those to the south. Similarly, we can also see how slow and, eventually, how minimal the influence of European material culture has been. In fact, for the years 1861 to 1891, the average proportion of births to deaths has been 39:40, going from 33:48 in 1860 to 44:35 in 1891.[50]

In Alaska, at the other end of the Eskimo region, we can see the same things. Our earliest information, which comes from the first Russian colonists, relates to the tribes of the south and is certainly neither very precise nor trustworthy and it allows only some vague estimates. But in Glasunov's travel diary we have more circumstantial data about the Eskimo of the Kuskokwim delta, where the maximum number of people per settlement was 250.[51] According to Petroff's[52] census (followed by a more reliable one by Porter which we will consider later),[53] the maximum density in this region was attained by the settlements on the Togiak River. On the other hand, the Kuskowigmiut[54] were the largest of all the known Eskimo tribes, though hardly the most densely settled, considering the area that they inhabited. It is worth noting that, like the Togiagmiut, this tribe settled beside rivers exceptionally rich in fish and, consequently, the people escaped certain dangers. Yet we must not exaggerate the importance of these relatively fortunate settlements. From Porter's lists, it seems that none of them reached the size indicated by Petroff. The Kassiamiut settlement which was reported by Petroff as having 605 individuals appears not to have been a proper settlement, but, rather, a collection of villages[55] which included a number of creoles and Europeans.[56] Another area where settlements are also larger and closer together is the group of islands situated between the Bering Strait and the southern part of Alaska.[57] And yet the density here, calculated on the basis of habitable land(?), is still very low: thirteen people per sq. kilometre.[58]

From all these facts it is apparent that there is a sort of natural limit to the size of Eskimo groups – a strict limit that may not be exceeded. Deaths or emigration – or the combination of these two factors – keep the Eskimo from exceeding this level. By their nature, Eskimo settlements are not large. One might almost say that the restricted size of their morphological unit is as characteristic of the Eskimo as their appearance or the common features of the dialects they speak. Thus, in the census lists, we can immediately recognize those settlements that have come under European influence or those that are not properly Eskimo: their scale noticeably exceeds the mean.[59] This applies to the so-called Kassiamiut settlement which we were just discussing; it is also true of that at Port Clarence which, in fact, serves as a station for European whalers.[60]

The composition of a settlement is just as characteristic as its size. It comprises few old people and few children; for various reasons, Eskimo women generally have only a small number of children.[61] The age pyramid rests, therefore, on a narrow base and it tends to thin sharply after sixty-five. On the other hand, the female population is considerable and, within this population, the position of widows is quite exceptional[62] (see Appendix 2). The high number of widows – especially remarkable, since celibacy is almost unknown and Eskimo men prefer to marry widows rather than young girls – is almost entirely because so many men die at sea. It is important to establish these facts, to which we will return later.

We must look to the Eskimo way of life for the causes of this situation. Indeed, this is not at all difficult to understand; it is, on the contrary, a remarkable application of the laws of biophysics and of the necessary symbiotic relation among animal species. European explorers have frequently insisted that, even with European equipment, there is no better diet nor better economic system in these regions than that adopted by the Eskimo.[63] They are governed by environmental circumstances. Unlike other arctic people, the Eskimo have not domesticated the reindeer;[64] instead they live from hunting and fishing. Game consists of wild reindeer which are found everywhere, musk oxen, polar bears, foxes, hares, some relatively rare fur-bearing carnivores, and various species of birds: ptarmigan, crows, wild swan, penguin and small owls. But catching these animals is, to some extent, a matter of luck, and for lack of suitable techniques they cannot be hunted in winter. Therefore except for passing birds or reindeer and some chance encounters, the Eskimo live chiefly off marine animals. Cetaceans form the principal source of their subsistence. In its important varieties, the seal is the most useful animal; where there are seal, one expects to find Eskimo.[65] Various species of the dolphin family, including the grampus and the white whale, are also actively hunted, as well as the walrus; the walrus mainly in the spring; the whale, even, in the autumn.[66] Marine and fresh-water fish and sea-urchins also form a small portion of the diet. By relying on the kayak in open waters or by patiently waiting at ice-holes, men are able to spear marine animals with their remarkable harpoons. And they eat their flesh either raw or cooked.

Three things are required by every Eskimo group: (1) in winter, a cover of ice; (2) in spring, open waters for hunting seal; and (3) in summer, a territory for hunting and fresh water for fishing.[67] These three conditions are found together only at places that are a variable distance from one another; they occur at fixed points and in limited number. Only in such places are the Eskimo able to settle. Nor do they ever settle on enclosed bodies of water:[68] they have definitely withdrawn from certain coasts which, to all appearances, were once open but have since become enclosed.[69] These three requirements have confined Eskimo settlements within strict limits, and an examination of some particular cases will indicate why this is so.

We may take, for example, the settlements at Angmagssalik,[70] which is situated on the eastern coast of Greenland at a relatively low latitude. The coast is blocked by ice as far as the 70° parallel. This mass of ice is maintained by the polar current that descends from Spitzbergen, passes through the Denmark Strait and goes on to Cape Farewell and Davis Strait. From the east, the coast is unapproachable; but at this relatively low latitude there is enough sunlight in summer to clear the sea over a sufficient area for hunting. Yet these conditions are unstable and precarious. The sea may not become ice-free; the supply of game animals is quickly exhausted and, on the winter ice, they are difficult to catch. Then again, the limited area of open water and the danger of icebergs which are continually being detached from the ice cap prevent groups from moving easily beyond the vicinity of the fiords. They must stay near those places that combine all the necessary conditions for their existence. If some accident occurs, or if one of their usual resources happens to fail, they cannot easily search a little further on for what they need. They must immediately move some distance to another likely spot, and these long migrations are not undertaken without great risks and without the loss of lives. We can see why, under these conditions, it would be impossible for groups to reach a large size. Anything that exceeds a certain limit, any imprudent modification of implacable physical laws or any unfortunate combination of weather conditions, has, as its fatal consequence, a reduction of the population. If the ice along the coast is late in melting, seal-hunting becomes impossible. If it melts too quickly because of a strong Föhn wind, then it is impossible to venture out in a kayak or to hunt on the ice: since it has begun to thaw, seal and walrus no longer surface. If people try to go north or south without all conditions being just right, then, sadly, the *umiak* (women's boat) with several families on board may sink.[71] If, driven to extremes, the Eskimo eat their dogs, they only increase their misery because travel by sledge over the snow and ice then becomes impossible.[72]

Let us move now to Point Barrow,[73] the northernmost point on the American coast. Here we see the same situation. Although the sea is rarely closed, it is also rarely free of ice. All the Europeans who have been there say that the marine and terrestrial game is *just* sufficient for the population. Hunting presents continual risks which the Eskimo know how to avert only by religious means; indeed, hunting is a constant danger which even the use of firearms has not yet eliminated. Population size is thus limited by the nature of things. It is so exactly in balance with food resources that these cannot diminish, however slightly, without causing a significant decrease in the population. From 1851 to 1881 the population was halved: this large reduction was the result of the fact that whale-hunting became less bountiful after the establishment of European whalers.[74]

To sum up, we can see that the limitation on Eskimo settlements depends on the way in which the environment acts, not on the individual, but on the group as a whole.[75]

2   Seasonal Morphology

We have now considered the general morphology of the Eskimo or, more specifically, the constant features of this morphology. But we know that this morphology also varies according to the time of year; we must now examine these variations, as these are the main concern of this study. Although the settlement is always the fundamental unit of Eskimo society, it still takes on quite different forms according to the seasons. In summer, the members of a settlement live in tents and these tents are dispersed; in winter, they live in houses grouped close to one another. Everyone, from the earliest authors onward,[1] who has had a chance to follow the cycle of Eskimo life, has observed this general pattern. First, we are going to describe each of these two types of habitat and the two corresponding ways of grouping. We shall then endeavour to determine their causes and their effects.

Summer habitat

The tent
We begin by considering the tent,[2] because it is a simpler construction than the winter house.

Everywhere, from Angmagssalik to Kodiak Island, the tent has the same name, *lupik*,[3] and the same form. In structure it consists of poles arranged in the shape of a cone;[4] over these poles are placed skins, mostly of reindeer, either as separate pieces or stitched together. These skins are held down at the base by large stones capable of withstanding the often severe force of the wind. Unlike Indian tents, Eskimo ones are not open at the top; there is no smoke that has to be allowed to escape, for their lamps produce none. The entrance can be closed tightly, and then the occupants are plunged in darkness.[5]

The normal type of tent naturally varies somewhat according to locality; but these variations are completely secondary. Where reindeer are rare,[6] as at Angmagssalik and throughout eastern Greenland, the tent is made of sealskin; since wood is scarce, the form of the tent is also somewhat different. It is placed in a spot with a steep slope[7] so that it leans against the earth; a horizontal beam supported in front by an angular frame is sunk in the ground and skins and thin laths are laid on this. The same conditions, remarkably enough, produce the same effects both among the Iglulik[8] on Hudson Bay and in the southern part of Baffin Land.[9] Since narwhal bones often replace wood, the tent has a form that is strikingly similar to that at Angmagssalik.

Rather than all these technological details, it is more important to know what kind of group lives in the tent. From one end of the Eskimo area to the other, this group consists of a family[10] defined in the narrowest sense of this word: a man and his wife (or, if there is room, his wives) plus their unmarried children including adopted children. In exceptional cases, a tent may include an older relative, or a widow who has not remarried and her children, or a guest or two. The relationship between the family and the tent is so close that the structure of the one is modelled on the structure of the other. It is a general rule, among all Eskimo, that there should be one lamp for each family; thus, ordinarily, there is only one single lamp to a tent.[11] Similarly, there is only one bench (or raised bed of leaves and branches at the back of the tent) covered with skins for sleeping; this bed has no partition to separate the family from any guests.[12] Thus the family lives perfectly united within this tightly closed interior; it builds and transports this summer dwelling which is made exactly to its measure.

Winter habitat

The house

As summer turns to winter, there occurs a complete change in the morphology of Eskimo society, in its mode of livelihood and in the structure of its sheltered groups. Eskimo dwellings do not remain the same; their population is different, and they are arranged in a completely different settlement pattern.

Instead of tents, Eskimo build houses,[13] and indeed long-houses,[14] as winter dwellings. We will begin by describing the external form of these houses and then proceed to discuss their content.

The Eskimo long-house is made up of three essential elements which serve to identify it: (1) a passage that begins outside and leads into the interior via a partially subterranean entrance; (2) a bench with places for lamps; and (3) partitions which divide the bench into a certain number of sections. These distinctive traits are specific to the Eskimo house; they are not found together in any other known type of house.[15] In different localities, however, houses may have particular characteristics which give rise to a certain number of secondary varieties.

At Angmagssalik,[16] houses are 24 to 50 feet long and 12 to 16 feet wide. They are constructed on land that generally has a steep slope (see Figures 1 and 2). The earth is excavated in such a way that the rear wall is at almost the same level as the surrounding land. This rear wall is somewhat larger than the

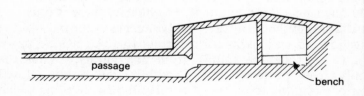

Figure 1 Cross-section of the house at Angmagssalik (Henri Beuchat).

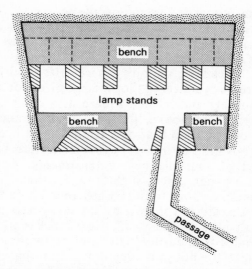

Figure 2 Floor plan of the house at Angmagssalik (Henri Beuchat).

wall that forms the front of the house. This arrangement gives the misleading impression that the house is below ground. The walls are of stone, or of wood covered with turf and often with skins; inner walls are almost always covered. In front and always at a right-angle with the wall is the passage whose entrance is so low that one can enter the house only on one's knees. Inside, the earth is covered with flat stones. At the rear of the house is a low continuous bench, from 4 to 5 feet wide and raised about 1½ feet from the ground. In Angmagssalik, it is actually supported by stones and turf, but elsewhere, in southern and western Greenland,[17] it rests on stakes; this is also the case in the Mackenzie region[18] and in Alaska.[19] This bench is divided into compartments by a short partition: each of these compartments, as we shall see, corresponds to a family and in the front of each of the compartments is placed the family lamp.[20] Along the front wall is another smaller bench which is reserved for adolescent unmarried young people or guests when they are not invited to share the family bed.[21] In front of the house are storage places for provisions such as frozen meat, props for boats and, sometimes, a kennel for the dogs.

In the Mackenzie region[22] where driftwood is abundant, houses are built entirely of logs: large pieces of wood resting on one another and set in a square with space on each side. When seen from above, the plan is more that of a star-shaped polygon than that of a rectangle, as is the case with the previous kind of house. A further difference is that it is composed of four distinct compartments. Each compartment has a bench that is slightly higher than the benches in houses in Greenland. In the compartment with the entrance, the bench is divided in two by the entry-way and, like the bench for guests in Greenland, these benches are reserved for guests and for utensils.[23] A final difference is that the passage into the house is even lower than that in Greenland and leads into the compartment which faces the sea, preferably towards the south[24] (see Figure 3).

In Alaska we find a house that is an intermediate type between the two preceding ones. The plan once more becomes rectangular,[25] as in Greenland, but it often consists of several rectangles grafted onto a single passage.[26] Since wood is also abundant throughout southern Alaska, the floor of the central rectangle is covered with planks. The only characteristic that appears to be specific to houses in this region is the arrangement of the passage; instead of leading into the house through one of the walls, it proceeds underground and ends up in the central portion of the house.[27]

It is easy to see how these different kinds of houses are merely variations on the same fundamental type, for which the Mackenzie house provides perhaps the closest approximation. The various materials that the Eskimo have at their disposal in the different regions are an important factor that contributes to determining these variations. Thus, at certain points in the Bering Strait,[28] in Baffin Land[29] and in the north-west region of Hudson Bay,[30] driftwood is rare or totally absent.[31] Here whale-ribs are used instead, but this results in a different kind of dwelling. The house is small, not very high, and is round or oval. The walls are covered with

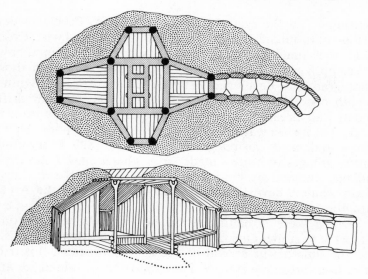

Figure 3 Floor plan and cross-section of the Eskimo house in the Mackenzie region. Both have been redrawn to our specifications because the drawings in Petitot (1876) are plainly inaccurate, while those in Franklin (1828) are incomplete.

skins which are overlaid with turf; over the walls there is a kind of dome. This is called the *qarmang*, and it has its own passage.

Let us suppose now that this last resource of the Eskimo builder, whale-ribs, were unavailable; then, other forms appear. The Eskimo often has recourse to a primary material that he knows is marvellously useful and is always at hand: namely, snow.[32] Thus the igloo or snow-house is found in Baffin Land[33] and along the northern coast of America.[34] The igloo has all the essential features of a large house: it is usually a multiple or composite house;[35] two or three igloos are linked and open onto the same passage; it is always dug into the earth and is always equipped with a passage whose entry is partially underground; and, finally, it contains at least two benches of snow with two places for lamps[36] (see Figure 4). We can also establish historically that the igloo is a substitute for the rectangular or polygonal house. In 1582, writing about the Meta Incognita Peninsula, Frobisher describes huts made of earth and turf.[37] A little later, Coats finds the same kind of hut further away.[38] At this time, however, both climate and currents were different from those that gradually developed between the sixteenth and nineteenth centuries.[39] It is therefore quite possible that driftwood was already rare in the sixteenth century, so rare, in fact, that its use was reserved for tools and weapons. Hence more and more *qarmang* were built. In 1829 Parry finds entire villages of houses made from whalebones.[40] But these villages themselves gradually became impossible as European whalers devastated the straits and bays of the Arctic archipelago.[41]

Where there is neither wood nor whalebones, the only resort is to stone. One tribe on Smith Strait attempted this.[42] At the time of the arrival of the first Europeans, this tribe was in a miserable state.[43] The expansion of inland ice and

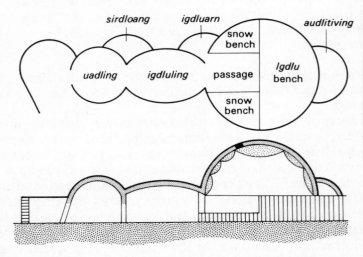

Figure 4 Floor plan and cross-section of a simple igloo from the north-west region of Hudson Bay (Henri Beuchat).
igdluling: *passage and recess for dogs.*
uadling: *cooking area and sump. The small side vaults are used for storing provisions.*

the persistence of drifting ice throughout most of the year not only put an end to the arrival of driftwood but obstructed large whales, and made it impossible to hunt whales, walruses and seals in open waters.[44] The bow, the kayak, the *umiak* and most of the sleds disappeared because of a lack of wood. These unfortunate Eskimo were reduced to such circumstances that they retained merely the memory of their former technology.[45] As a result they were forced to build their houses completely of stone and turf. Because of the nature of these materials, the form of the house was modified. Since large stone houses were too difficult to build for this destitute population, they had to be satisfied with small ones.[46] Yet despite these changes there is still an evident connection between these houses and the main type of large house. In its essential features, the small house resembles the large Greenland house. It is basically a miniature of this large house: the entrance is under the ground, the window is in the same place, the bench is raised in the compartments.[47] Finally and most important, the house is often inhabited by several families. This, as we shall see, is the distinctive feature of a long-house.

This small stone house is, therefore, a transformation of the large house of Greenland and the Mackenzie region. Some archaeologists have, however, argued the contrary, namely that the small house was the prototype for the large one. The only evidence for this hypothesis is the fact that in north-west Greenland on the one hand, in Franz-Josef Land, Scoresby Sound[48] and the Parry Archipelago[49] on the other, old winter settlements have been found which appear to have consisted of small stone houses similar to those at Smith Strait. But this single piece of evidence is hardly convincing. Elsewhere there are numerous ruins of large houses. These houses are all relatively uniform[50] and there is nothing to prove that these ruins are not, in fact, the oldest remains of winter houses that we possess. Furthermore, if the small house had been the initial form, it would be difficult to account for the generality and permanence, under various guises, of the large house type.[51] One would have to claim that, at some specific but unspecified time and for equally unspecified reasons that are difficult to perceive, the Eskimo changed their winter settlement pattern from isolated families to a collective family structure. There is no plausible reason for this transformation, whereas we have shown how the reverse transformation can easily be explained in the case of the tribe at Smith Strait.

The contents of the house

Now that we know something about the arrangement of the house, we can consider the nature of the group living in it.

Just as the tent consists of a single family, so the winter dwelling, in all its forms, normally contains several families.[52] We have already seen this from the previous discussion. The number of families who live together, however, is somewhat variable. There can be as many as six,[53] seven or even nine families among the tribes of eastern Greenland,[54] and formerly ten in western Greenland,[55] though the number decreases to two for small snow-houses and for the tiny stone houses at Smith Strait. The existence of a certain number of families in the same house is so characteristic of Eskimo winter settlements that, wherever this begins to diminish, it is a sure sign that the culture itself is waning. Thus, in the census reports from Alaska, it is possible to distinguish Eskimo villages from Indian villages according to the number of families per house.[56]

In the Greenland house, each family has its own set place. In the igloo, each family has its own special bench;[57] similarly, the family has its own compartment in the polygonal house,[58] a section of a partitioned bench in houses in Greenland[59] and its own side in the rectangular house.[60] There is thus a close relationship between the structure of the house and the structure of the group that it shelters. It is interesting, however, to note that the space occupied by each family is not proportional to the number of its members. Families are considered as separate units, each equivalent to the other. A family consisting of a single individual occupies as much space as a large one comprising more than two generations.[61]

The kashim

Besides these private dwellings, there is another winter construction which deserves particular attention because it highlights particular features of Eskimo life during the winter season. This is the *kashim*, a European term derived from an Eskimo word meaning 'my place of assembly'.[62]

The *kashim*, it is true, is no longer to be found in all areas. It is, however, still found throughout Alaska[63] and among all the tribes of the western coast of America as far as Point Atkinson.[64] According to the accounts we have of the most recent explorations, it is still found in Baffin Land, along the north-west coast of Hudson Bay and on the southern coast of Hudson Strait.[65] Its existence was noted by the very first Moravian missionaries to Labrador.[66] In Greenland, with one dubious exception,[67] there is no trace of the *kashim* in the ruins of former settlements, nor is it mentioned by the early Danish writers; yet the *kashim* is still remembered in some Eskimo tales.[68] There are good reasons, therefore, to regard it as a normal part of every primitive Eskimo settlement.

The *kashim* is an enlarged winter house. The connection between the two constructions is so close that the diverse forms of the *kashim* in different regions parallel the various forms of the winter house. There are two essential differences. First, the *kashim* has a central hearth, whereas the winter house does not, except in the extreme south of Alaska where the influence of the Indian house has its effect. This hearth is found not only where the use of firewood offers a good practical reason for its existence,[69] but also in temporary *kashim* made of snow, as in Baffin Land.[70] Second, there are usually no compartments, and often no benches but only seats, in the *kashim*.[71] Even when it is built of snow and it is therefore impossible to construct a single large dome because of the nature of the material to hand, domes are joined together and walls are shaped to give the *kashim* the form of a large pillared hall.

These differences in the arrangement of the interior correspond to differences in function. There are no divisions or compartments but only a central hearth because the *kashim* is the communal house of the entire settlement.[72] This, according to reliable sources, is where the ceremonies take place that reunite the community.[73] In Alaska, the *kashim* is more specifically a men's house,[74] where adult men, married or unmarried, sleep apart from the women and children. Among the tribes of southern Alaska, it serves as the sweat-house;[75] but this use of the *kashim* is probably relatively recent and of Indian, or even Russian, origin.

The *kashim* is built exclusively during the winter. This is itself good evidence that it is the distinctive feature of winter life. Winter is characterized by an extreme concentration of the group. This is not only the time when several families gather together to live in the same house, but all families of the same settlement, or at least the men of the settlement, feel the need to reunite in the same place to live a communal life. The *kashim* was created in response to this need.[76]

The seasonal distribution of dwellings

This discussion is intended to provide a better understanding of the seasonal arrangement of Eskimo dwellings. These are different in their form and dimensions and, as we have seen, they shelter groups of very different sizes. But their distribution is also very different in summer and winter. According to whether it is winter or summer, they are either gathered together or scattered over a vast territory. The two seasons present two entirely opposed appearances.

The distribution of winter dwellings

While the internal density of each separate house varies, as we have shown, according to the region, the density of an entire settlement is always as high as subsistence factors permit.[77] The social volume of a settlement – the area actually occupied and exploited by the group – is kept to a minimum. Seal-hunting, which requires hunters to go out a certain distance, is carried out exclusively by men, and they do not proceed beyond the shore except for brief and limited purposes; and although the sled-trips undertaken mainly by men[78] may be important, they hardly affect the total density of a settlement except when it becomes overcrowded.[79]

The same is true at Angmagssalik where the group is as concentrated as possible; there an entire settlement resides in a single house which, consequently, comprises all the members of the social unit. Although normally a house may have from two to eight families, the house at Angmagssalik has a maximum of eleven families with a total of fifty-eight occupants. Along the coast-line of 120 miles, there are, in fact, thirteen such settlements with thirteen houses. The 392 inhabitants of the region are divided among these houses, with an average of thirty people per house.[80] This extreme concentration is not, however, the original situation but undoubtedly the result of an evolution.

In all other cases where scattered and isolated winter houses have been observed, they were apparently inhabited by families who, for various reasons, had separated from their original group.[81] The 'single houses' observed by Petroff in Alaska[82] seem virtually to disappear in Porter's census; and, in any case, the first major census for this region – that by Glasunov in 1824 which was fortunately conducted during the winter – mentions only villages with eight to fifteen houses comprising 200 to 400 members.[83] Among the ruins of the Parry Archipelago and of North Devon Island winter settlements are frequently found reduced to a single house, but this reduction, considerable as it may seem by comparison with average settlements, is hardly surprising in view of the fact that these ruins evidently date from a period when impoverished Eskimo were abandoning these regions.[84]

So we can say that, in general, once we have eliminated the seemingly contrary evidence, a winter settlement is composed of several houses near one another.[85] These houses were not systematically arranged,[86] except – as far as we know – for two cases among the southern tribes of Alaska.[87] This fact is important.

This arrangement of dwellings is enough to demonstrate the concentration of the population at this period. But perhaps this concentration was once greater. Given the present state of our knowledge, this conjecture can hardly be rigorously proved, but it is certainly plausible. In fact, early English voyagers describe Eskimo villages dug into the earth like molehills, with all the huts grouped around a central hut that was larger than the rest.[88] This was, in all probability, the *kashim*. On the other hand, for the tribes to the east of the Mackenzie, there are specific statements about communications between the houses and even between the houses and the *kashim*.[89] Thus the winter group could be considered as having once consisted of a kind of large house that was both a single and a multiple unit. This would explain the formation of settlements later reduced to a single house, such as at Angmagssalik.

The distribution of summer dwellings

In summer, the distribution of the group is totally different.[90] Winter density gives way to a contrary phenomenon. Not only does each tent contain only a single family, but these tents are greatly separated from one another. The gathering of families into one house and of houses into one settlement is followed by a dispersion of families; the group scatters. At the same time, the relative immobility of winter gives way to travel and migrations that are often quite considerable.

This dispersion takes different forms according to local circumstances. Usually, families spread out both along the coast and into the interior. In Greenland, with the sudden arrival of summer,[91] families who were concentrated in the igloos of the settlement load the *umiaks* with the tents of two or three associated families. In a very short time, all the houses are empty and the tents are strung out along the shores of the fiord. They are ordinarily located at a considerable distance from one another.[92] At Angmagssalik, opposite the thirteen winter houses (each of which, we know, forms a settlement), twenty-seven tents are scattered over the islands of the fiord; these are later moved to at least fifty different sites – the rare pastures where the reindeer graze (see Figure 5). According to Cranz's superb reports,[93] in the coastal area between the settlement of Neu Herrnhut and Lichtenfels there was just as great a dispersion; for eight settlements at most, there were no fewer than twenty-two halting-places and camp sites. And undoubtedly Cranz is mistaken in underestimating, rather than overestimating, their number. Besides the dispersion along the fiords,[94] the Eskimo in Greenland also made trips to the grazing sites of reindeer and to salmon rivers.[95] The same was true in Labrador.[96]

We have good information on the expansion of the Iglulik in Parry's time, thanks to excellent Eskimo maps which he published;[97] these show the summer dispersion of the tribe. This small tribe stretches over a coastal area of more than sixty halting-places and even swarms inland along the rivers

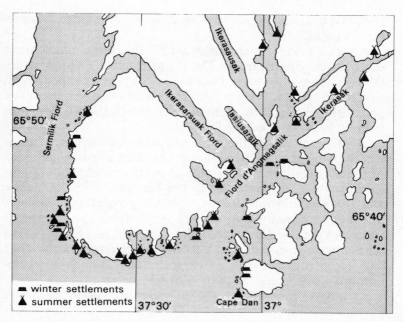

Figure 5 The winter settlements and summer settlements at Angmagssalik (Henri Beuchat).
This map is based on Holm (1894, p. 249). The contours of the coastlines of the fiords are still uncertain; see S. Rink (1900, pp. 22, 23 and 43).

and lakes of the interior, with some families going in search of wood to the other side of the Melville Peninsula and right across Baffin Land. When one realizes that these seasonal migrations are undertaken by families and may require six to twelve days' travel, it is apparent that this mode of dispersion implies an extreme mobility of groups and individuals.[98] According to Boas,[99] the Oqomiut, who live in the north of Baffin Land, crossed Lancaster Strait when the ice was breaking up and then went on up to Ellesmere Land as far as Smith Strait. In any case, it is certain that the former settlements in the northern part of Devon Island were equally widely dispersed; for eight winter settlements, there are ruins of thirty summer sites scattered over an immense coastline. These examples could be multiplied. Figure 6 shows the areas of dispersion covered by three tribes in Baffin Land.

All along the American coast,[100] the same phenomena occur in varying degrees. The Point Barrow Eskimo attain the maximum distance in their two-stage trading expeditions: first they go to Icy Cape to obtain European goods; then they go to Barter Island to exchange these with the Kupungmiut Eskimo of the Mackenzie.[101]

The three deltas or the three estuaries are the only regions where patterns of dispersion are less than normal, but each of these exceptions is the result of particular chance circumstances which we can note. In the Mackenzie,[102] the Yukon and the Kuskokwim regions, summer groups are relatively large. One account mentions 300 people from the Mackenzie tribe who gathered at Cape Bathurst.[103] But this group, at the time it was observed, had gathered only temporarily; they had come together for an exceptionally abundant whale-hunt, of white whales in particular.[104]

At other times during the summer this same tribe was

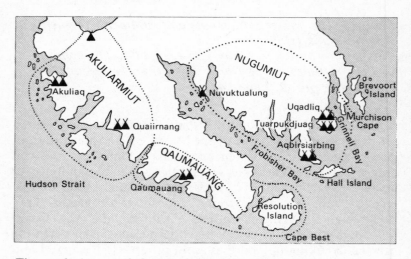

Figure 6 Areas of the summer dispersion of the Akuliarmiut, the Qaumauang and the Nugumiut. Only winter settlements are shown; the two single triangles indicate the furthest locations of summer tents (Henri Beuchat).

dispersed. It is also reported that, in certain villages of the Kuskokwim, the winter houses are occupied during the summer; but it seems clear that they are occupied only temporarily, when the group had gone to the sea to take part in exchanges, and then returned to disperse upstream to fish for salmon and later out onto the tundra to hunt reindeer and migrating birds.[105] Elsewhere, especially in villages on maritime rivers, it happens that before abandoning the winter houses, the village sets up its tents or its winter houses in a regular order not far away.[106] But there is a specific reason for this particular situation which includes the fact that the population density does not fall below its winter level:[107] in both summer and winter, the group maintains virtually the same subsistence pattern based on a diet of fish. It is indeed interesting to note that, even in this awkward situation, a dual morphology persists, despite the fact that the group remains in one place and the reasons for its summer dispersion have disappeared.[108]

This summer dispersion must be considered in relation to an aspect of Eskimo collective mentality whose analysis provides a better understanding of what makes this summer organization so different from that of winter. Ratzel has distinguished between the *geographical volume* and the *mental volume* of societies.[109] The geographical volume is the space actually occupied by a particular society; its mental volume is the geographical area that the society succeeds in encompassing in its thought. Thus there is a marked contrast between the modest dimensions of a poor Eskimo tribe and the immense stretches over which it spreads, or the enormous distances covered by central tribes in the interior.[110] The geographical volume for the Eskimo is the area covered by their summer groups. But how much more remarkable is their mental volume, in other words the extent of their geographical knowledge. Instances of long trips undertaken by sledge before the melting of the snow in spring, by families in *umiaks* during the summer or by individuals in winter are not at all uncommon.[111] As a result, the Eskimo, even those who have not made these trips, have a traditional knowledge of extremely distant areas; all explorers have relied on this geographical talent, with which Eskimo women are also eminently endowed.[112] We ought, therefore, to consider Eskimo summer society not just as a society that extends over a vast area in which it lives and travels but as a society that thrusts well beyond this area families or isolated individuals – lost children, as it were – who return to their natal group when winter comes or during the next summer, having wintered where they could. One could compare these individuals with the long antennae extended forward by a creature that is itself extraordinarily distended.

3 The Causes of Eskimo Seasonal Variations

It would be rather difficult to discover all the causes that resulted in the establishment of the various features of this twofold organization, for they happened in the course of a historical development that was probably quite long and during a migration of extraordinary scope. Yet we would like at least to indicate some of the factors that underlie this phenomenon, if only to distinguish social causes from others of a limited and purely physical nature.

Most observers have usually been satisfied with simple explanations. They note that the communal house[1] and the quasi-subterranean one retain heat better, that the presence of a number of individuals under the same roof is enough to raise the temperature, and that the clustering of several families economizes on fuel. They thus see in this organization nothing more than a means of fighting the cold. Yet, though there is some truth to these notions, they are only partial explanations. First, it is inaccurate to say that the Eskimo inhabit the coldest regions of the world.[2] A certain number are settled in relatively temperate regions; for example, in the south of Greenland or Labrador, where the major difference between summer and winter is a result of the proximity of the inland ice or of the ice that is carried by the glacial stream rather than of any real lowering of temperature. Second, the Indians of the interior of Labrador, the Montagnais, the Cree of the Barren Grounds[3] and the Indians of the Alaskan forest,[4] live in higher latitudes and experience conditions of a continental climate that is basically harsher than that of their coastal Eskimo neighbours. Yet these Indians all live in tents throughout the year and though their tent is similar to that of the Eskimo, the opening at its top – the smoke-hole, with which the Eskimo are unacquainted – makes it a great deal less efficient against the cold, even in summer. It is thus surprising that the Indians have not borrowed from their neighbours an invention as useful as the house. This is just another piece of evidence to contradict those theories that suppose that they have accounted for a social institution by showing from whom it has been borrowed. Third, where there are good reasons for altering the form of the house, these alterations have not taken place; this can be taken as evidence that the winter house is, as it were, a distinctive feature of Eskimo society. Thus, in the forested districts of Alaska, some tribes have gone beyond the shores of the rivers and have their winter settlements closer to the woods than to the seal-hunting grounds. But instead of installing a hearth of wood and opening their roofs to allow the smoke to escape, these tribes prefer to purchase oil for their lamps, at considerable expense,[5] from those of their neighbours who have some.

One explanation that shows an awareness of this problem and its complexity is that proposed by Steensby.[6] He has argued that primitive Eskimo culture was once an Indian type of culture whose closest approximation can still be observed among the Eskimo during the summer; on the other hand, the form of the Eskimo house corresponds to the same type as that of the Plains Indians (from the Mandan to the Iroquois). The house is supposedly the result of primitive borrowing and was developed, along with the whole of the winter technology, at a time when the Arctic Ocean began to approach and overtake the Eskimo. But nowhere do we find a single trace of any Eskimo group whose principal occupation was hunting and whose only dwelling was the tent. From the moment that the Eskimo appear as a specific social group, they already have their well-established two-fold culture. Thus the oldest summer settlements are always near the oldest winter settlements. Moreover, any comparison between an Indian long-house and an Eskimo house is relatively inexact, for in an Indian long-house there is neither a passage, nor benches, nor places for lamps –

the three characteristic traits of an Eskimo house.

We must therefore put aside these explanations and see how we might otherwise account for the concentration of the Eskimo in the winter and their dispersion in the summer.

We have already seen how strongly the Eskimo are attached to their way of life, however poor it may be. They can hardly conceive of the possibility of leading another kind of existence. Never do they seem to have made an effort to modify their technology. Neither the examples they see of neighbouring peoples with whom they have contact, nor the clear prospect of a better life, is enough to induce in them the desire to change their ways. Some Eskimo in the northern part of America have carried on a steady commerce with their neighbours, the Athapascans and Algonquins. If they had adopted the snowshoe from these Indians instead of retaining their waterproof boot, small groups of Eskimo would have been able to pursue animals in the middle of the winter that they were unable to stop in their summer migration.[7] But the Eskimo keep so much to their traditional organization that they hardly dream of changing.

It is by means of this technology, a social phenomenon, that Eskimo social life becomes a veritable phenomenon of symbiosis that forces the group to live like the animals they hunt. These animals concentrate and disperse according to the seasons. In winter, walruses and large numbers of seals assemble at certain points along the coast. The seal needs a sheet of ice to protect its young and also a spot where the ice is open for as long as possible in order to come and breathe easily at the surface; the number of these spots near shoals, beaches, islets and capes is fairly restricted, despite the great expanse of coastline. It is only at these points, at this time, that it is possible to hunt seal, given the technology of the Eskimo. On the other hand, as soon as the water is open and 'leads' appear, the seals move and disperse to frolic in the sea, in the depths of the fiords and below the steep cliffs, and the hunters must spread out in the same way to reach them, for it is quite exceptional for seals to congregate. At the same time, the opportunities to fish in fresh water for salmon and other smaller sorts of fish and to hunt deer and reindeer[8] in the high pastures or in the delta tundras lead to a nomadic life and a scattering in pursuit of game. During the summer, this dispersion is just as easy for the Eskimo as it is for their Indian neighbours, for they do not need snowshoes to follow and pursue the animals. As for river fishing, they do this precisely at those points where game are known to pass.[9]

In summary, summer opens up an almost unlimited area for hunting and fishing, while winter narrowly restricts this area.[10] This alternation provides the rhythm of concentration and dispersion for the morphological organization of Eskimo society. The population congregates or scatters like the game. The movement that animates Eskimo society is synchronized with that of the surrounding life.

Nevertheless, although biological and technological factors may have an important influence, they are insufficient to account for the total phenomenon. They provide an understanding of how it happens that the Eskimo assemble in winter and disperse in summer. But they do not explain why this concentration attains that degree of intimacy which we have already noted and which the rest of this study will confirm. They explain neither the reason for the *kashim* nor the close connection that, in some cases, seems to unite it to other houses. Eskimo dwellings could supposedly be grouped together without concentrating on this one point and without giving birth to the intense collective life which we will consider when we examine the effects of this organization. Neither need they have been long-houses. The natives could have placed their tents side by side, covered them better, or they could have constructed small houses instead of living in family groups under the same roof. One ought not to forget that the *kashim*, or men's house, and the large house where several branches of the same family reside are not confined to the Eskimo. They are found among other peoples and, consequently, cannot be the result of special features unique to the organization of these northern societies. They have to be related, in part, to certain characteristics that Eskimo culture has in common with these other cultures. These characteristics cannot be investigated here; the question, by its very generality, goes beyond the framework of this study. But the state of Eskimo technology can only account for the time of the year when these movements of concentration and dispersion occur, their duration and succession, and their marked opposition to one another.[11]

4 The Effects of Eskimo Seasonal Variations

Now that we have described the seasonal variations of Eskimo morphology and have established some of their causes, we must study their effects.[1] We will examine the way in which these variations affect both the religious and legal life of the group. This we consider to be a significant part of this study.

Effects on religious life

The religion of the Eskimo has the same rhythm as their social organization. There is, as it were, a summer religion[2] and a winter religion; or rather, there is no religion during the summer. The only rites that are practised are private, domestic rituals: everything is reduced to the rituals of birth[3] and death[4] and to the observation of certain prohibitions. All the myths that (as we shall see) fill the consciousness of the Eskimo during the winter appear to be forgotten during the summer. Life is that of the layman. Even magic, which is often a purely private matter, hardly appears except as a rather simple sort of medical science[5] whose rituals are minimal.

By contrast, the winter settlement lives in a state of continuous religious exaltation. This is the time when myths and legends are transmitted from generation to generation. The slightest event requires the more or less solemn intervention of the magicians, the *angekok*.[6] A minor taboo can be lifted only by public ceremonies[7] and by visits to the entire community.[8] At every possible opportunity these events are turned into impressive performances of public shamanism to avert the famine that threatens the group, particularly during the months from March to May when hunting is unreliable[9] and provisions are either dangerously low or have been exhausted. One can thus describe winter life as one long celebration. Earlier writers report perpetual dancing among the Eskimo of Greenland,[10] dancing that was certainly mainly religious. Even if we take into account mistaken observations and comments, what these writers tell us is probably further evidence of this non-stop religious life. The religious mentality of the group is carried to such an extreme in several Eskimo societies[11] that an exceptionally rigorous watch is kept for any religious failings. Any collective mishap – a storm that lasts too long, the escape of a game animal, an unfortunate break in the ice and so on – is attributed to the violation of some ritual prohibition. Such transgressions have to be publicly confessed so that their effects may be mitigated. The practice of public confession is indicative of the kind of holiness that marks the whole of winter social life.[12]

Not only is this religious life intense,[13] it also has a very special character which contrasts with life during the summer: it is pre-eminently collective. By this, we do not simply mean that festivities are celebrated in common, but that the feeling which the community has of itself and its unity suffuses all its actions. Festivities are not only collective in the sense that very many individuals assemble to take part; they are the object and the expression of the group.

This derives from the fact that they take place in the *kashim*,[14] wherever there is one, and, as we have already seen, the *kashim* was once probably found everywhere. Whatever its other features may be, it is always essentially *a public place* that manifests the unity of the group. This unity is indeed so strong that, inside the *kashim*, the individuality of families and of particular houses disappears; they all merge in the totality of the society. In fact, in the *kashim*, individuals are not grouped by families or by houses but according to certain barely differentiated social functions which they perform.[15]

The nature of the rituals that are celebrated during these festivities are an expression of the same character. This is notably the case with the so-called 'Bladder Festival' which is performed in Alaska and particularly among the Unalit of St Michael's Bay.[16] At the start, numerous masked dances are performed before the entire community, who sing. Then, at the very end, at one go, the bladders of all the sea animals killed *by the entire group* during the year are thrown into the sea. The souls of the animals, which these bladders are believed to contain, go back to be reincarnated in female seals and walruses. By this single ritual, the winter settlement as a whole ensures its continued subsistence.

Another festivity, the feast of the dead, has also been observed among these same Unalit,[17] although its equivalent appears to be found in all Eskimo territories.[18] It consists of two essential parts. Since it is customary that the latest child to be born takes the name of the last person who has died, the feast begins with a request to the souls of the dead to become reincarnated for a short time in the namesake which each of the dead has in the settlement. Next, these living namesakes of the dead are laden with presents, gifts are exchanged among all who have assembled, and then the souls are dismissed and they leave their human dwellings to return to the land of the dead. Thus, at this time, the group not only regains its unity but sees itself re-formed, through this same ritual, as an ideal group composed of all successive generations from the earliest times. Mythic and historic ancestors, as well as the recent dead, come to mingle with the living and all are in communion through the exchange of gifts.

The winter solstice festivals have the same significance. Among the central[19] and eastern Eskimo, the essential ritual consists – or, at least, once consisted – in extinguishing and then *simultaneously* relighting all the lamps of the settlement. When we note that the fire was certainly relit from a single fire produced by friction, we can see in this a kind of collective fire ritual.

We should add that these different festivities are always and everywhere accompanied, quite significantly, by the phenomenon of sexual licence, a subject to which we will return when we come to discuss personal status.[20] Communal sex is a form of communion, perhaps the most intimate form there is. When it occurs, it produces a fusion of individual personalities – something which we can see is far removed from the state of individualization and isolation in which small family groups live dispersed, during the summer, along enormous extents of coast.

This opposition between summer life and winter life does not, however, find expression simply in rituals, festivities and various sorts of religious ceremonies; it also profoundly affects ideas, collective representations and, in short, the entire mentality of the group.

In the course of a complex of festivities, among the Oqomiut of Baffin Land and the Nugumiut of Frobisher Bay,[21] the population divides into two teams. The one comprises all those born during the winter; they have a special collective name and are called the *axigirn*, the 'ptarmigans'. The other is composed of all those born during the summer, who are called *aggirn*, the 'ducks'. The former represent the land; the latter the sea. Each team tugs on a rope and, depending on who is victorious, either summer or winter will prevail. This division of the population into two groups, according to the season when they were born, is not restricted to this special ritual; it forms the basis of other customs among all the central Eskimo. During their lifetime, but particularly during the festivities that we have just mentioned, individuals wear an amulet made from the skin of the animal, generally a bird, that presides over the month of their birth.[22] It would seem from this tendency to classify people according to the season when they were born that the land birds are probably the winter birds and the sea birds are summer birds.[23] At Angmagssalik[24] (which is, however, far from where these practices are observed) birth rituals certainly vary considerably depending on whether they involve a 'winter' child or a 'summer' child. If a child is born during the summer, his first meal consists of soup made from some land animal, or from a river fish cooked in fresh water; the 'winter' child's first meal is soup from some sea animal cooked in salt water.

This division of people into two great categories appears indeed to be connected with an even greater and more general division that embraces all things. Without even discussing a number of myths in which all animals and important natural events are divided into two groups – one of winter, the other of summer[25] – we can recognize this same idea as the basis of many ritual prohibitions. There are winter things and summer things, and the Eskimo feel the opposition between these two fundamental classes so deeply that to mix them in any way is forbidden.[26] In the central regions, the skin of the reindeer (a summer animal) may not be brought into contact with the skin of the walrus (a winter animal); the same applies to the various objects used to hunt these two kinds of animals.[27] When summer has begun, an Eskimo may not eat caribou (a summer animal) until he has put away all his winter clothes and put on new ones, or at the very least, until he has put on clothes that were not used during the walrus-hunting season.[28] The small tents that shelter hunters during the summer are supposed to be buried under rocks along with the hunters' clothes; they are considered *shongeyew* or 'taboo'.[29] No covering or thong of walrus-skin should be brought to any of the places where reindeer are hunted, on pain of returning empty-handed. Winter clothes, if made of caribou-skin, have to be completed before the men can leave to hunt walrus.[30] Throughout the time the people are living on the ice, no one may work any skin, either caribou or reindeer.[31] Neither should salmon meat, a product of summer fishing, come into contact with the flesh of any sea animal, not even in the stomach of the faithful. By contrast, contact with seal-meat is less strictly regulated since these animals are hunted throughout the year and at the same time as other animals. The violation of any of these taboos imparts to the offender a defilement that is visible to the game and is communicated by contagion to all who approach that person. Thus the game withdraw and famine follows throughout the land.[32] In fact, the existence of these taboos has necessitated the formation of a special class of messengers whose task is to announce the capture of the first walrus.[33] This is the sign that winter has begun. All work on caribou-skins immediately ceases. The way of life changes completely.

Thus the way in which both men and objects are classified bears the imprint of this fundamental opposition between the two seasons. Each season serves to define an entire class of beings and objects. We have already seen the basic role of this classification on the mentality of the people. One could say that the concept of summer and the concept of winter are like two poles around which revolves the system of Eskimo ideas.[34]

Effects on jural life

The object of a legal system is to regulate the possible material relations among members of one society. Whether this involves the respective rights and duties of persons in relation to one another (the regulation of persons) or of persons in relation to those objects appropriated by the group or by individuals (the regulation of goods), these various legal and moral institutions are merely the collective manifestation of the necessary conditions of communal life.[35] Thus we ought to expect this twofold morphology to have an even greater influence on Eskimo jural life than on religious life. We shall see, in fact, that there is one set of laws for the winter and another for the summer,[36] and that each reacts upon the other.

The family

We do not propose here to make a study of the Eskimo family, but we will show that the principal features of Eskimo domestic organization are a function of the twofold morphological organization that we have described.

The kinship terms for the family provide one of the surest ways for determining the relations that unite various members of the same domestic group. These terms can be studied with relative ease thanks to the schedules published by Dall and Morgan,[37] although they are rather sketchy. At first sight, it would appear that there are two kinds of family: one in which kinship is collective, conforming to the type that Morgan called classificatory, and the other in which kinship is individualized. There are two indications of the first type. In the descending line, the term *eng-ota* is applied to grandchildren, as well as to individuals who are more distantly related either consanguineally or by adoption; in other words, to the children of the nephews and cousins of the son's generation. Similarly the terms *e-tu-ah* and *ninge-o-wa* apply not only to grandparents (consanguineal or adoptive) but also to their brothers and sisters and to all kin of their generation. In the collateral line, cousins of various degrees are not distinguished from other relatives and bear a designation that identifies them with the inhabitants of the house.[38] In short, no degree of kinship, male or female, is distinguished except for the following relatives: father, mother, son, daughter, father's brothers and sisters and mother's brothers and sisters and their children. Thus within a family in which kinship relations are extended but undifferentiated, there appears another highly restricted unit in which kinship is, on the contrary, individualized.

These two sorts of domestic organization recognizable in Eskimo kinship nomenclature actually exist: one is the summer family,[39] the other the winter family. And since each has a different composition, each is governed by its own appropriate rules.

The rules for the summer family are relatively patriarchal. The predominant role is held by the father as *provider*,[40] and by male children of hunting age. They are more than just heads of the family; they constitute its very foundation. Their disappearance would necessarily result in the *complete* disappearance of the family; the young children, if they were not adopted within another tent, would be put to death.[41] The mother's role, it must be added, is no less important. Were she to disappear, the family would also be entirely destroyed.[42] These two persons are so indispensable that, even when the children are somewhat older, if a husband loses a wife or a wife her husband, he or she will try to remarry as quickly as possible. The existence of this group is therefore extremely precarious: it rests entirely on one or two persons. This configuration of the family is a specific characteristic of Eskimo culture and unique to it. In short, the conjugal pair is an essential element of the family, just as in more developed cultures; and this fact is even more remarkable, given the fragility of the conjugal bond.

Other features confirm this specific character of the summer family. There is, first, the relative dominance of the head of the family, the *igtuat*, in Greenland.[43] He has the absolute right of command, even over his adult sons; and it seems that cases of disobedience are remarkably rare. He determines the movements of the group and the division of meat.[44] He has the absolute right of punishment, even over his wife; but he is wary of abusing it because, although he can repudiate her, she, in turn, is equally able to abandon him.[45]

The organization of the paternal family is usually linked to the need for descendants and this characteristic is also true of the Eskimo family. This need is even greater among the Eskimo than among other peoples, as the existence of old people without children is impossible. Without adult sons willing to hunt for them, especially during the summer, elderly couples cannot survive.[46] This is particularly true of elderly widows, who cannot remarry or be adopted in the same way as young children. Moreover, at least in some instances, this need for descendants can take on a religious aspect. The elderly know that they have to be reincarnated after their death in the bodies of their namesakes – the newly-born children of the settlement; and the veneration given to their spirits through the person of this representative depends upon their children. Consequently the lack of a child, whether legitimate or adopted, could jeopardize their spiritual existence.[47]

During the winter the rules of domestic life are entirely different. The nuclear family, so clearly individualized during the summer, tends to disappear to some extent within a much wider group, a kind of joint-family which resembles that of the Zadruga Slavs, and which constitutes domestic society *par excellence*: this is the group who together occupies the same igloo or long-house.[48]

The individuals who live under the same roof are bound not just by economic relations but by genuine moral ties; this is clear from the kinship relations that the terminology has already revealed.[49] There is a term for designating these kin: they are *igloq atigit*,[50] 'house kin', a term which Danish and English observers have appropriately translated as *husfaeller* or *housemates*, and which designated *all cousins*. There is formal evidence that, together, these 'housemates' form an individual's closest circle of kin after his immediate family.[51] In fact, wherever we come across what we take to be the most primitive type of Eskimo house, the group who inhabits it consists of consanguineal kin with their affines. Thus, at Utiakwin (Point Barrow),[52] despite a state of social disintegration, one long-house comprised a man, his wife and adopted daughter, two married sons, each with his wife and child, a widowed sister with her son and daughter-in-law plus the latter's grand-daughter. The quasi-genealogical tables we possess show that the principles for the recruitment of members of a household are appreciably the same in other areas.[53]

A particular feature of this special kinship relation is the prohibition of marriage among *housemates*; at least, this seems to be the rule. For it is generally forbidden to marry one's full cousins;[54] we know that these bear the same name as the *housemates*, who are usually brothers and sisters and the descendants of these brothers and sisters who live together during the winter. So, where there is a question of a prohibition among kin, observers may have been mistaken; whereas it is clearly the case in Greenland that individuals brought up in the same house are forbidden to marry.[55] The oldest texts that we have report this fact and they appear to link closely kinship relations between first cousins and among the members of a long-house. There is thus a kind of special fraternity that imparts an incestuous character[56] to sexual unions between members of the same igloo. Two pieces of evidence, however, appear to contradict this rule. Nelson explicitly states that, among the Unalit of St Michael's Bay,[57] first cousins do marry and Holm mentions the frequent exceptions at Angmagssalik to the rule that one must look for a wife outside the house.[58] But we must not forget that at Angmagssalik, where each settlement consists of a single house, the confusion between the long-house and the winter settlement has altered the most essential feature of this organization. Angmagssalik is an exceptional case and it is hardly surprising that it does not conform strictly to the rule. Since everyone in the settlement lives under the same roof, it was obviously necessary to permit marriage among cohabitants and consequently the prohibition had to give way. On the other hand, the first cousins whom Nelson describes may very well belong to different houses or even to different settlements.[59] Since this case has to do with the only tribe that is reported to have totemic clans,[60] cousins who are allowed to marry may perhaps be members of two clans that maintain *connubium*.

The large winter family is not only composed differently from the summer family, but it is also organized on other principles: it is not a patriarchal family. The head[61] is designated not by birth but because of certain personal characteristics. He is generally an old man, a good hunter or the father of one; a rich man, often the owner of an *umiak*; an *angekok* or magician. His powers are not extensive; his functions are to receive strangers and to distribute places and portions of meat. He is asked to regulate internal differences. But his rights over his companions are, in the end, quite limited.

Moreover, beyond the circle of the extended family, there is yet another grouping that appears only in winter; this is the settlement itself. We can reasonably inquire whether the settlement constitutes a kind of large family, or a clan.[62]

We have already noted that all the inhabitants of the same settlement are designated by a special term which shows that very specific moral bonds exist among them. Danish writers translate this term as *bopladsfaeller* or *place-fellows*.[63] The existence of the *kashim* among all Eskimo (except those of Greenland and Labrador where it certainly did once exist) is further evidence that all the men of a settlement form one united society that is genuinely fraternal.[64] Finally, the fact that, at Angmagssalik, the house merges with the winter settlement is another indication of how close the relations within the long-house are to those that unite different families in a winter settlement. If one admits the hypothesis – even where the house is not completely merged with the settlement – that different houses were originally closely connected to one another and to the *kashim*,[65] the preceding remarks will have more general significance.

Yet whatever the particular facts may be, everything about the moral regulation of the winter settlement confirms the fact that individuals are steeped in a family atmosphere. The settlement is more than a simple accumulation of houses or an exclusively political and territorial entity; it is also a domestic unit. All its members are united by strong bonds of affection, analogous to those which, in other societies, unite different families within a clan. The rules of the settlement are not just the sum of the rules of each household; the settlement has its own rules which are reminiscent of large family gatherings.

Beginning with the earliest writers and continuing until Nansen, who wrote his observations in verse, most observers[66] have been struck by the gentleness, intimacy, and general gaiety that reigns in an Eskimo settlement. A kind of affectionate good feeling seems prevalent among everyone. Crimes appear to be relatively rare.[67] Theft is almost non-existent, though there are few occasions where theft could be committed, given the rules over property.[68] Adultery is almost unknown.[69]

One of the characteristic features of a clan is the extreme indulgence shown toward offences or crimes committed by its members: sanctions are principally moral. This same indulgence is found in an Eskimo settlement.[70] Homicide, when it occurs, is often deemed an accident.[71] Individuals whose violent behaviour makes them dangerous are considered to be mad and, if they are killed, that is the reason.[72] The only sanction applied within the settlement, at least in Greenland, is an instance of this good-natured attitude: this is the famous 'singing duel'. In this tambourine dance, [73] two adversaries – plaintiff and defendant – take turns insulting each other using rhymed verse and refrain, until the fertile inventiveness of one of the opponents assures him a victory over the other. The esteem of the onlookers is the only reward, their reproach the only punishment to constitute this unique judgment.[74] The Eskimo winter settlement is, therefore, a marvellous example of the Arab definition of a clan: *the place where there is no blood vengeance*.[75] Even public crimes are generally the object of only moral punishment. Except for malevolent magic,[76] which is more often attributed to the people of a neighbouring settlement,[77] there seem to be no crimes that are sanctioned in any other way. Even serious breaches of ritual prohibitions, some of which are believed to endanger the life of the entire society,[78] are not punished, in the central regions,[79] except by acknowledgment, confession and imposed penances. This mild repression is evidence of the familial intimacy that reigns within the group.

Such intimacy is sharply opposed to the isolation maintained between neighbouring settlements. 'Place-fellows' were obliged to avenge each other's deaths when the aggressor belonged to another locality.[80] Tales are told of numerous vendettas in Greenland between one settlement and another.[81] Sources indicate that throughout Baffin Land and to the north-west of Hudson Bay there used to be actual wars.[82] In eastern Greenland, Holm and Hanserâk report a similar hostility and constant enmity between settlements on different fiords.[83] In Greenland,[84] in Baffin Land, King William Land,[85] and at one time in Alaska[86] as well, the ceremonies for receiving a stranger regularly consisted of exhibitions of fighting. It is claimed, undoubtedly with some exaggeration, that when a group visited a neighbouring settlement, the duel or violent game[87] which took place between two chosen champions ended in the death of one of the combatants.

Yet the best evidence of genuine kinship among members of the same settlement is the custom of exchanging women.[88] This is reported in almost all Eskimo societies. These exchanges take place in winter between all the men and all the women of the settlement. In some cases, in western Greenland for example, the exchange was formerly restricted to married couples.[89] Generally, however, all nubile indivi-duals take part. Usually this practice is associated with collective winter festivities,[90] but sometimes, notably in Greenland, there is no connection. There, at least in those regions that have not been influenced by Christianity, this old custom survives in its entirety. At a certain time, the lamps are put out and actual orgies take place.[91] But we have very little information on whether particular women are assigned to particular men,[92] except for two cases that are quite typical. In the masked festivities at Cumberland Sound[93] that we have already mentioned, one of the masked figures representing the goddess Sedna pairs men and women solely according *to their names*, without taking into account their kinship relations. In this way, men and women are joined as the ancestors were once joined, since they bear the names of the mythic ancestors and are their living representa-tives. The same practice is reported in Alaska,[94] and appears to be indicated elsewhere. Thus, at this moment, the entire organization of the nuclear family and of the household disappears along with the normal regulation of sexual relations: all particular groupings are subsumed within the total group that makes up the settlement. Its mythic organization, reconstituted for a brief period, effaces all other groups. For a brief time, one can say, the clan in all its formlessness[95] absorbs the family.

These general exchanges take place among all the members of the group and form a kind of sexual ritual. And there are other more or less permanent exchanges of women contracted between individuals for specific reasons.[96] Some occur in the winter house;[97] others are contracted just before the group disperses in June[98] for the summer season and are accompanied by an exchange of gifts.[99] Both, however, seem to take place only among members of the same settlement. At Smith Strait,[100] they frequently occur during the first years of marriage and can be contracted only between specific individuals.[101] Later they may occur for short periods between any member of the Cape York tribe, who constitute a kind of 'single family'.[102] Alaska is the only region where exchanges are reported to occur between members of different settlements.[103] But this exception proves the rule. In fact, the men who make these exchanges become brothers by adoption; the women who are exchanged are considered to be each other's sisters; and the same applies to all the children born from these unions.[104] Relations formed in this way are, in all respects, identical to those that derive from natural kinship relations.[105] This is, therefore, further evidence that the groups who practise communal sex are groups of kinsmen, since when such exchanges occur among strangers, they create bonds of kinship.

In short, the only feature of a clan that a settlement does not possess is a rule of exogamy. Nansen[106] believed that the settlements at Angmagssalik amounted to exogamous clans. Unfortunately, this conclusion seems to have been based exclusively on Holm's reports, which referred to houses and not to settlements. Moreover, other documents that Holm has provided, including the genealogy of a single family with members in various settlements along the fiord, show that a person can easily marry within the settlement where he lives.[107] Marriage is, however, prohibited among all the original inhabitants of a settlement and is permitted only when one of the parties happens to be living in a settlement other than that in which he or she was born. Yet it is worth noting that the only author to mention totemic clans among the Eskimo says nothing about exogamy.[108]

Thus, in both domestic and religious life, the contrast between summer and winter is as accentuated as possible. In summer, the Eskimo family is no more extended than our own. In winter, this small family is reabsorbed into much larger groups; another type of domestic unit is formed and takes precedence. This is the large family of the long-house; the settlement becomes a kind of clan. We could almost describe the Eskimo as two different peoples and, if we were to consider only the two jural structures of their society, the Eskimo could be classified under two separate categories.

Effects on the regulation of property

Seasonal variations affect property rights even more significantly than they affect personal rights and duties. There are two reasons. First, the objects used vary according to the seasons; food and implements are entirely different in winter and in summer. Second, the material relations that link individuals to one another vary both in number and in kind.[109] Alongside a twofold morphology and technology there is a corresponding twofold system of property rights.

In summer, individuals and nuclear families live isolated in their tents; at most, they may gather in temporary camps. There is no communal hunting, except for whales, and each daring fisherman or adventurous hunter either brings his prize to his tent or stores it in his 'cache' without having to consider anyone else.[110] The individual is therefore as sharply distinguished as the small family. We can see also that there are clearly two, and only two, categories of objects: the category appropriated by the individual and that appropriated by the family.[111]

Individual property consists of the following objects: clothes and amulets; then the kayak and the weapons which are naturally owned exclusively by men. Generally a woman owns her own family lamp,[112] soapstone cooking pots and a collection of utensils. All these household objects are identified, in a magical or religious way, with individual persons.[113] Eskimo are reluctant to lend, give or exchange objects that have already been used;[114] they are buried with the dead.[115] In Alaska and perhaps generally, certain objects, notably weapons, bear property marks.[116] These marks serve a double purpose: they permit the recognition of objects and retain a portion of the magical power of their owner.[117] An object is always part of an individual and the individual cannot be separated from it. Something can be sold or bartered only if a portion of it is retained[118] or if it is licked clean by its owner.[119] With this precaution, Eskimo can part with their possessions without having to fear that the buyer will exert an evil power over them by means of the object. It is, however, worth noting that this strict identification of an individual with an object is confined to objects of Eskimo manufacture.[120]

The property that belongs to the nuclear family is even more limited. It owns no fixed property and only a few portable objects. Even the lamp is the wife's property.[121] The family has nothing of its own except its tent, coverings and sledge.[122] The women's boat or *umiak*, which is used to carry the tent on summer migrations and in whale-hunting, may perhaps belong to this same class of goods; perhaps, however, it belongs more specifically to those families that gather together in the winter.[123] In any case, it is clear that the furnishings of the nuclear family are associated exclusively with summer life, or with that portion of summer life that carries on into winter. But the rights of the family are incontestable as far as food is concerned. The hunter must bring back his entire catch to his tent, no matter how far away he is or how hungry he may be.[124] Europeans have marvelled at how strictly this rule is observed. Game and the products that can be extracted from it do not belong to the hunter, but to the family, no matter who hunted it. This remarkable altruism makes a strange contrast to the cold indifference shown to the injured and infirm;[125] once they are incapable of keeping up with the family in its migrations, they are abandoned.[126]

The rules for winter are completely different. In contrast

to the egoism of the individual or the nuclear family, a generous collectivism prevails.

First, there is communal regulation of fixed property. The long-house belongs to none of the families who live in it; it is the joint property of all the 'housemates'. It is built and repaired jointly.[127] Even land appears to be collectively appropriated.

Collective rights over food, instead of being limited to the family as in the summer, extend to the entire house. Game is divided equally among all members.[128] The exclusive economy of the nuclear family totally disappears. The family may not put aside for its own use food from its own hunting or from the share of meat it receives. External stocks such as the frozen provisions that are brought from distant catches are joint property. Provisions that were gathered earlier and are brought in later are shared to meet common needs.[129]

Communal law is, however, asserted even more within the settlement than in the long-house. The opposition to the individual and patriarchal summer rights is most accentuated in this regard.

First, the land occupied by the settlement is joint property: no one, not even an ally, can settle on this land without the tacit approval of the community.[130] And, of course, the *kashim*, where there is one, is also common property.[131]

Then the collective consumption of food is even more marked within the settlement than within the long-house. Certain tribes divide all game among everyone, not just in times of want but at all times.[132] The winter life of the Eskimo thus involves a continual round of communal feasts.[133] Whenever large animals like walruses and small whales are caught, they provide the occasion for general feasting; and the distribution of meat is carried out in the most egalitarian way. Stranded or captured whales are cut up by the entire group. Everyone in the district is invited;[134] everyone takes what he can, and, according to the curious custom in Greenland, the injuries inflicted on people during this sort of scramble are not punishable.[135]

Rights over movable property held either by individuals or families fade quite readily in the face of a kind of general and latent communal right. When something is lent, there is a moral obligation to return it, but it may not be reclaimed.[136] Restitution must be made voluntarily. If, however, an object is lost by the person who borrowed it, it does not have to be replaced.[137] As we have already explained, under these conditions theft is rare—indeed it is almost impossible.

Moreover, in Labrador, Greenland and the central regions, it is a general rule that a family ought to possess only a certain amount of wealth.[138] Throughout Greenland, when the resources of a house surpass what is considered to be the normal level, this wealth must be given to poorer individuals. Rink reports that the members of a settlement jealously watch to see that no one possesses more than anyone else.[139] When this occurs, the surplus, which is arbitrarily determined, is turned over to those who have less. This abhorrence of possessing too much is also widespread in the central regions.[140] It is especially noticeable in the ritual exchange of presents during the festival of Sedna,[141] when gifts are given to the namesakes of the ancestral dead,[142] to children[143] and to visitors.[144] Combining this ritual with Indian traditions from the north-west coast results in an institution, among Alaskan tribes, that is certainly not identical with but definitely similar to an Indian potlatch.[145] The majority of villages in this region have chiefs[146] of a sort, with vaguely defined authority; or at least these villages have a number of rich and influential men. But the community remains jealous of their power; hence, a chief can remain a chief, or rather a rich man can remain rich and influential, only if he distributes his goods periodically. Only the benevolence of his group allows him to accumulate his wealth and, by dispersing this wealth, he triumphs over it. Or, alternatively, he enjoys his fortune and makes reparation for it; this expiation is a condition of that enjoyment. Nelson describes chiefs who were assassinated because they were too rich.[147] Moreover, a mystic efficacy is attributed to these exchanges and to this redistribution: they are necessary for success in hunting; for without generosity there can be no luck.[148] This economic communism of winter is strikingly parallel to the sexual communism during this same season; it shows, once more, the degree of moral unity that the Eskimo community attains at this time.

The interaction of the two jural systems

Despite the opposition that exists between these two moral and jural systems, they do not affect each other simply because they occur successively within the same society and the same men take part in both. During the winter, an Eskimo cannot entirely let go of habits or ways of perceiving and acting to which he has become accustomed during the summer and vice versa. It is therefore quite natural that some of the customs and institutions of one season should continue into the following season.

The nuclear family of the summer is not totally abolished within the long-house. The various families who have gathered together retain some of their individuality. The house is common to all, but each occupies a separate place in it. In the Greenland house, families are separated by partitions;[149] in the houses of the western region, each family has its own compartment;[150] in the snow-house of the central Eskimo, each has its side of the igloo or its own small igloo.[151] Each family has its own lamp for cooking, and each is free to depart or to rejoin others when the time comes to leave or to resume their winter quarters.[152]

Another institution that has the same origin is adoption.[153] The Eskimo are one of the peoples who have made the most use of this practice,[154] but it would be neither possible nor useful, if the winter group retained its unity throughout the year. On the one hand, orphan children as members of a large egalitarian family are supposed to be raised by the entire community; whereas, on the contrary, accounts and folk tales[155] throughout the Eskimo area are unanimous in their description of the sad situation of the orphan. On the other hand, for the same reason, if the nuclear family did not periodically replace the large family, there would be no cause for married couples without children to be concerned about their future material[156] and spiritual welfare. They would feel no need to adopt some young relative or stranger to care for them when they were old and, later, for their spirits.[157]

The winter family also has an effect on the summer family – and the morals of the one affect the other. In the long-house an Eskimo does not wear clothes, nor does he wear clothes in his tent, even when it is cold. A feeling of shame at this is simply unknown.[158] In spite of the isolation and individualism of the summer family, a rule of generous hospitality[159] is maintained – doubtless a carry-over from the intense collective life of winter. In some cases, a guest is even allowed to sleep with the family.[160] This right appears to be the special prerogative of kinsmen of the same winter house or companions in the same settlement.

The same kind of interaction can be seen in regard to property rights. We have already noted that, within the longhouse, each family has its own lamp and coverings; each individual has his weapons and clothes. Even the rules by which meat from the hunt is divided among members of a house bear hints of the individualistic rights of the summer. Here[161] the hunter himself divides the meat and graciously invites his companions to take their share, rather than making this an obligatory exchange. Elsewhere[162] either the owner of the animal or the order in which meat is apportioned is fixed by a set of rules that indicate a kind of compromise between the two conflicting rights: the head of a seal, for example, goes to the person who harpooned it or who delivered the last blow; then come the other hunters, and finally kinsmen. In other areas there are no restrictions on the absolute right of 'housemates' over the animal.

These interactions demonstrate that, in many respects, the resemblances between the two systems of rules are the result of some sort of survival. Without these reciprocal effects, the opposition between the two seasons would be even sharper and this would mean that all individualistic elements in Eskimo culture would occur during the summer and all communal elements during the winter.

No matter how one assesses the relative importance of these extreme differences and their mutual influences, it is still the case that Eskimo law, in its totality, accords with, and only with, a twofold morphology.

5 Conclusion

The social life of the Eskimo assumes two clearly opposed forms which parallel a twofold morphology. Undoubtedly, between the two, there are transitions: a group does not always abruptly take up winter quarters nor leave them; similarly, a small summer camp is not always composed of one single family. But it still is generally true that the Eskimo have two ways of grouping, and that in accordance with these two forms there are two corresponding systems of law, two moral codes, two kinds of domestic economy and two forms of religious life. In the dense concentrations of the winter, a genuine community of ideas and material interests is formed. Its strong moral, mental and religious unity contrasts sharply with the isolation, social fragmentation and dearth of moral and religious life that occurs when everyone has scattered during the summer.

The qualitative differences that distinguish these successive and alternating cultural patterns are directly related to quantitative differences in the relative intensity of social life at these two times of the year. Winter is a season when Eskimo society is highly concentrated and in a state of continual excitement and hyperactivity.[1] Because individuals are brought into close contact with one another, their social interactions become more frequent, more continuous and more coherent; ideas are exchanged; feelings are mutually revived and reinforced. By its existence and constant activity, the group becomes more aware of itself and assumes a more prominent place in the consciousness of individuals.

Conversely in summer, social bonds are relaxed; fewer relationships are formed, and there are fewer people with whom to make them; and thus, psychologically, life slackens its pace.[2] The difference between these two periods of the year is, in short, as great as can possibly occur between a period of intense social activity and a phase of languid and depressed social life. This shows quite clearly that the winter house cannot be accounted for exclusively in technological terms. It is obviously one of the essential elements of Eskimo culture, appearing when the culture attains its maximum development; it becomes an absolutely integral part of it, and disappears when the culture begins to decline.[3] The winter house is, therefore, dependent on this entire culture.

Social life among the Eskimo goes through a kind of regular rhythm. It is not uniform during the different seasons of the year. It has a high point and a low point. Yet though this curious alternation appears most clearly among the Eskimo, it is by no means confined to this culture. The pattern that we have just noted is more widespread than one would at first suspect.

First, among the American Indians, there is an important group of societies, quite considerable in themselves, that live in the same way. These are mainly the tribes of the north-west coast:[4] Tlingit, Haida, Kwakiutl, Aht, Nootka and even a great number of Californian tribes such as the Hupa,[5] and the Wintu. Among all these peoples there is an extreme concentration in winter and an equally extreme dispersion in summer, though there exist no absolutely necessary biological or technological reasons for this twofold organization. In keeping with this twofold morphology there are very often two systems of social life. This is notably the case among the Kwakiutl.[6] In winter, the clan disappears, giving way to groups of an entirely different kind: secret societies or, more exactly, religious confraternities in which nobles and commoners form a hierarchy. Religious life is localized in winter; profane life is exactly like that among the Eskimo in summer. The Kwakiutl have an appropriate saying for expressing this opposition:[7] 'In summer, the sacred is below, the profane is on high; in winter, the sacred is above, the profane below.' The Hupa show similar variations which were probably more marked than they are today. Many

Athapascan societies, ranging from those in the far north such as the Ingalik and Chilcotin, to the Navaho of the New Mexican plateau,[8] also have the same character.

These American Indian societies are not, however, the only ones that conform to this type. In temperate or extreme climates where the influence of the seasons is clearly evident, there occur innumerable phenomena similar to those we have studied. We can cite two particularly striking cases. First, there are the summer migrations of the pastoral mountain peoples of Europe which almost completely empty whole villages of their male population.[9] Second, there is the seemingly reverse phenomenon that once regulated the life of the Buddhist monk in India[10] and still regulates the lives of itinerant ascetics, now that the Buddhist *sangha* no longer has followers in India: during the rainy season, the mendicant ceases his wandering and re-enters the monastery.

What is more, we have only to observe what goes on around us in our western societies to discover these same rhythms. About the end of July, there occurs a summer dispersion. Urban life enters that period of sustained languor known as *vacances*, the vacation period, which continues to the end of autumn. Life then tends to revive and goes on to increase steadily until it drops off again in June. Rural life follows the opposite pattern. In winter, the countryside is plunged into a kind of torpor; the population at this time scatters to specific points of seasonal migration; each small local or familial group turns in upon itself; there are neither means nor opportunities for gathering together; this is the time of dispersion. By contrast, in summer, everything becomes reanimated; workers return to the fields; people live out of doors in constant contact with one another. This is the time of festivities, of major projects and great revelry. Statistics reflect these regular variations in social life. Suicides, an urban phenomenon, increase from the end of autumn until June, whereas homicides, a rural phenomenon, increase from the beginning of spring until the end of summer, when they become fewer.

All this suggests that we have come upon a law that is probably of considerable generality. Social life does not continue at the same level throughout the year; it goes through regular, successive phases of increased and decreased intensity, of activity and repose, of exertion and recuperation. We might almost say that social life does violence to the minds and bodies of individuals which they can sustain only for a time; and there comes a point when they must slow down and partially withdraw from it. We have seen examples of this rhythm of dispersion and concentration, of individual life and collective life. Instead of being the necessary and determining cause of an entire system, truly seasonal factors may merely mark the most opportune occasions in the year for these two phases to occur. After the long revelries of the collective life which fill the winter, each Eskimo needs to live a more individual life; after long months of communal living filled with feasts and religious ceremonies, an Eskimo needs a profane existence. We know, in fact, that the Eskimo are delighted with this change, for it seems to come as a response to a natural need.[11] Undoubtedly, the technological factors which we have noted account for the order in which these alternate movements succeed one another during the year; but if these factors did not exist, this alternation would still perhaps take place, though in a somewhat different way. One fact would tend to confirm this viewpoint. When favourable circumstances such as a major whale catch or the possibility of a large market bring the Eskimo of the Bering Strait and of Point Barrow together in the summer, the *kashim* temporarily reappears.[12] And with it come all the ceremonies, wild dancing, feasts and public exchanges that usually take place there. The seasons are not the direct determining cause of the phenomena they occasion; they act, rather, upon the social density that they regulate.

The climacteric conditions of Eskimo life can be accounted for only by the contrast between the two phases of the year and the clearness of their opposition. As a result, among these people, the phenomenon is so easily observed that it almost springs to view, but very likely it can be found elsewhere. Furthermore, though this major seasonal rhythm is the most apparent, it may not be the only one; there are probably other lesser rhythms within each season, each month, each week, each day.[13] Each social function probably has a rhythm of its own. Without wishing for a moment to offer these speculations as established truths, we believe that they are worth mentioning,[14] for they offer serious possibilities for fruitful research.

Whatever the value of these remarks, however, there is another general conclusion to this work that deserves the same attention.

We have proposed, as a methodological rule, that social life in all its forms – moral, religious, and legal – is dependent on its material substratum and that it varies with this substratum, namely with the mass, density, form and composition of human groups.[15] Until now, this hypothesis has been verified in only a few important cases. It has been shown, for example, how the respective evolution of criminal and civil law depends on a society's type of morphology;[16] how individual beliefs develop or decline depending on the degree of integration or disintegration of familial, religious or political groups;[17] and how the mentality of primitive tribes directly reflects their social organization.[18] But the observations and comparisons upon which these laws depend allow some room for doubt that may apply *a fortiori* to the general principle that we initially stated. The phenomena we have studied could well be dependent on other unknown factors in addition to morphological variations. Eskimo societies, however, offer a rare example of a test case which Bacon would have regarded as crucial. Among the Eskimo, at the very moment when the form of the group changes, one can observe the simultaneous transformation of religion, law and moral life. This case has the same clarity and precision as an experiment would have in a laboratory and it is repeated every year with an absolute invariability. Henceforth we can say that this sociological proposition is relatively established. Therefore the present study has, at least, this methodological advantage: it has shown how the analysis of one clearly defined case can establish a general law better than the accumulation of facts or endless deduction.[19]

Appendix 1

The Kuskokwim District[a]

Villages or settlements	Population	Houses	Families
Aguliagamiut	94	7	15
Agumak	41	6	8
Ahgomekhelanghamiut	15	1	3
Ahgulakhpagamiut	19	2	4
Ahguliagamiut	106	6	22
Ahpokagamiut	210	11	44
Ahguenach-Khlugamiut*	6	1	1
Akiagamiut	97	7	20
Akiakchagmiut	43	5	8
Annovokhamiut	15	1	2
Apahichamiut	91	7	18
Askinaghamiut	138	14	33
Atchalugumiut	39	6	9
Bethel*	20	4	6
Chalimiut	358	17	58
Chechinamiut	84	7	16
Chimingyangamiut	40	2	7
Chokfoktoleghagamiut	18	2	4
Chuligmiut	32	3	7
Chuligmiut (upper)	30	2	7
Dununuk	48	5	15
East Point, no. 1	36	3	9
East Point, no. 2	41	3	8
Ekaluktalugumiut	24	2	7
Etohlugamiut	25	5	6
Gilakhamiut	22	1	3
Ighiakchaghamiut	81	4	15
Ingeramiut	35	3	9
Kalukhtugamiut	29	2	5
Kahmiut	40	3	8

81

The Kuskokwim District[a]—cont.

Villages or settlements	Population	Houses	Families
Kailwigamiut	157	7	30
Kaltkagamiut	29	3	8
Kanagamiut	35	3	8
Kanagmiut	41	3	7
Kashuhnamiut	232	20	49
Kaviaghamiut	59	4	11
Kenaghamiut	257	10	54
Kennachananaghamiut	181	8	29
Kikikhtagamiut	119	11	25
Kinegnagamiut	92	7	19
Kinegnagmiut	76	6	17
Kl-changamiut	49	3	9
Klutagmiut	21	2	6
Kochlogtogpagamiut	20	2	3
Kolmakovsky*	26	4	6
Koot	117	8	22
Settlements of the			
River Koot	74	6	16
Kuskohkagamiut	115	7	23
Kwichampingagamiut	25	6	6
Kwigamiut	43	6	9
Lagoon, no. 1	30	3	7
Lagoon, no. 2	36	4	8
Lomavigamiut	53	5	13
Mumtrahamiut	162	11	33
Mumtrekhlagamiut	33	4	6
Napaimiut	23	2	6
Napaskeagamiut	97	5	12
Noh-Chamiut	28	6	6
Novokhtolamiut	55	3	11
Nunachanaghamiut	135	9	30
Nunavoknak-chlugumiut	107	5	21
Oh-hagamiut	36	4	9
Queakhpaghamiut	75	4	12
Quelelochamiut	112	6	20
Quiechlochamiut	83	7	16
Quiechlochagamiut	65	6	17
Quilochugamiut	12	2	2
Quinhaghamiut	109	6	20
Shinyagamiut	7	1	2
Shovenagamiut	62	4	14
Tefaknagamiut	195	10	33
Tiengaghamiut	60	4	13
Tulukagnagamiut	17	2	6
Tuluksagmiut	62	4	14
Tunaghamiut	71	5	14
Ugavigamiut	57	7	16

Villages or settlements		Population	Houses	families
Ugokhamiut		68	6	14
Ulokagmiut		27	7	7
Vinisahle*		140	23	28
Woklchogamiut		19	1	4
	Total	5,681	434	1,148

[a] Porter (1893, p. 164: table 6). The Eskimo of this region are gregarious. For those areas where they are least concentrated, see Porter (1893, p. 174). The average figure of 2.65 families per house is too low if we exclude Vinisahle, an Ingalik village; Bethel, a Mission; Kolmakovsky, a factory and summer house, as well as the other non-Eskimo settlements whose names appear with an asterisk.

Appendix 2

Age and Status of the Inhabitants of the Kuskokwim District [a]

Age (years)	Population			Unmarried			Married			Widowed		
	Total	Male	Female	Total	Male	Female	Total	Male	Female	Total	Male	Female
Under 1	84	48	36	84	48	36	—	—	—	—	—	—
1 to 4	739	380	359	739	380	359	—	—	—	—	—	—
5 to 9	651	323	328	651	323	328	—	—	—	—	—	—
10 to 14	535	278	257	532	278	254	2	—	2	1	—	1
15 to 19	727	301	426	498	296	202	217	5	212	12	—	12
20 to 24	703	358	345	228	176	52	429	175	254	46	7	39
25 to 29	564	322	242	60	47	13	424	253	171	80	22	58
30 to 34	404	207	197	12	11	1	319	177	142	73	19	54
35 to 39	316	160	156	—	—	—	223	134	89	93	26	67
40 to 44	246	103	143	1	—	1	171	78	93	74	25	49
45 to 49	246	131	115	2	2	—	151	94	57	93	35	58
50 to 54	163	81	82	—	—	—	88	55	33	75	26	49
55 to 59	107	56	51	—	—	—	59	37	22	48	19	29
60 to 64	105	57	48	—	—	—	53	42	11	52	15	37
65 to 69	20	10	10	—	—	—	12	8	4	8	2	6
70 to 74	7	3	4	—	—	—	3	2	1	4	1	3
75 to 79	10	6	4	—	—	—	6	4	2	4	2	2
80 to 84	8	4	4	—	—	—	3	3	—	5	1	4
85 to 89	4	2	2	—	—	—	—	—	—	4	2	2
90 to 94	—	—	—	—	—	—	—	—	—	—	—	—
95 to 99	—	—	1	—	—	—	—	—	—	—	—	—
100 to 104	1	—	—	—	—	—	—	—	—	1	—	1
Total	5,640	2,830	2,810	2,807	1,561	1,246	2,160	1,067	1,093	673	202	471

[a] Porter (1893, p. 175). Some of the data, as for example the woman who is over 100, are both improbable and unverifiable. On the other hand, Porter does not distinguish between Eskimo and Indians, but one can make corrections for this by using the figures in Petroff (1884, pp. 13–15).

Notes

Translator's Foreword

1 The translations to which I refer are (1) É. Durkheim, *Sociology and Philosophy*, translated by D. F. Pocock with an introduction by J. G. Peristiany, Cohen & West, London, 1953; (2) M. Mauss, *The Gift*, translated by I. Cunnison with an introduction by E. E. Evans-Pritchard, Cohen & West, London, 1954; (3) R. Hertz, *Death and the Right Hand*, translated by R. and C. Needham, with an introduction by E. E. Evans-Pritchard, Cohen & West, London, 1960; (4) É. Durkheim and M. Mauss, *Primitive Classification*, translated with an introduction by R. Needham, University of Chicago Press, 1963; (5) H. Hubert and M. Mauss, *Sacrifice*, translated by W. D. Hall with a foreword by E. E. Evans-Pritchard, Cohen & West, London, 1964; (6) C. Bouglé, *Essays on the Caste System*, translated with an introduction by D. F. Pocock, Cambridge University Press, 1971; (7) M. Mauss and H. Hubert, *A General Theory of Magic*, translated by R. Brain with a foreword by D. F. Pocock, Routledge & Kegan Paul, London, 1972. To this group should, perhaps, be added M. Granet, *The Religion of the Chinese People*, translated with an introduction by M. Freedman, Basil Blackwell, Oxford, 1975. Although not a formal contributor to the *Année sociologique* in its early phase, Granet was an eminent student of Durkheim and an intimate academic associate of Mauss, Davy and Bouglé.

2 Louis Dumont, who was lecturer in Indian sociology at the Institute, was particularly instrumental in promoting interest in the works of the *Année* school. My title quotation is taken from a lecture he gave in Oxford in 1952 which was later published in French as 'Une science en devenir' in *L'Arc 48: Marcel Mauss*, Aix-en-Provence, 1972, pp. 6-21.

3 E. E. Evans-Pritchard, Introduction to R. Hertz, *Death and the Right Hand*, p. 9.

4 Two invaluable sources on the development of the social sciences in

85

France and on the position of Durkheim and his school are T. N. Clark, *Prophets and Patrons: The French University and the Emergence of the Social Sciences*, Harvard University Press, 1973, and S. Lukes, *Émile Durkheim, His Life and Work: A Historical and Critical Study*, Allen Lane, London, 1973; Penguin Books, Harmondsworth, 1975.

5 In their intellectual division of labour, Mauss investigated the nature of exchange, Davy the contractual bonds created by exchange. Davy published his findings in a lengthy monograph, *La Foi jurée: Étude sociologique du problème du contrat, la formation du lieu contractuel*, Alcan, Paris, 1922.

6 Both title-page and table of contents of the ninth volume of the *Année sociologique* assign exclusive authorship of this essay to Mauss. The first and last pages of the essay, however, attribute authorship to Mauss with an underline noting that the essay was written 'avec la collaboration' of Beuchat. The precise nature of this collaboration is difficult to determine, although we know from some brief published notes on Mauss's seminar on the Eskimo (1903-4) in which Beuchat participated that his interests were in Eskimo migrations, morphology and technology. His collaboration is, thus, most clearly indicated in chapter 2 where he is, in fact, given explicit credit for maps and drawings. On the other hand, a final footnote absolves him of any responsibility for the editing and correcting of proofs. These indications, as well as the evidence of other research and writings of the two men, make it abundantly clear that this is primarily and predominantly a work by Mauss himself.

7 Nelson H. H. Graburn and B. Stephen Strong, *Circumpolar Peoples: an Anthropological Perspective*, Goodyear Publishing Co., Pacific Palisades, 1973, p. 171.

8 See Edmund Leach, *Culture and Communication*, Cambridge University Press, 1976, p. 3.

9 Richard B. Lee, '!Kung Spatial Organization: an Ecological and Historical Perspective' in R. B. Lee and I. DeVore, *Kalahari Hunter-Gatherers*, Harvard University Press, 1976. For a recent study of Eskimo seasonal variations, see David Damas, 'Characteristics of Central Eskimo Band Structure' no. 5, *National Museums of Canada Bulletin* 228, Ottawa, 1969, pp. 116-38.

10 With the establishment of a sixth section devoted to social morphology, a seventh section was created to retain diverse items. This gradually took on a more or less definitive form and came to include (1) Aesthetic Sociology (vol. 3), (2) Technology (vol. 4) and (3) Language (vol. 5). The subsection on language was added when A. Meillet joined the group.

11 *L'Année sociologique*, vol. 2, 1899, p. 520.

12 'Le sol, la société et l'état', *L'Année sociologique*, vol. 3, 1900, pp. 1-14.

13 See Durkheim's letter to Simiand dated 15 February 1902 which is quoted in S. Lukes, *Émile Durkheim*, Penguin Books, Harmondsworth, 1975, p. 295.

14 'Divisions et proportions des divisions de la sociologie', *L'Année sociologique*, n.s., vol. 2, 1927, reprinted in Marcel Mauss, *Oeuvres*, vol. III, pp. 178-245, ed. Victor Karady, Éditions de Minuit, Paris, 1969.

15 Ibid., p. 178.

16 Ibid., p. 178.

17 Ibid., p. 180.

18 Ibid., pp. 205-7.

19 See Mauss, *Manuel d'ethnographie*, Payot, Paris, 1947, p. 10.

20 See V. Karady, 'Présentation' to M. Mauss, *Oeuvres*, vol. I, p. xliv.

21 See Mauss, *Oeuvres*, vol. III, pp. 73-4.

22 *L'Année sociologique*, vol. 7, 1904, pp. 225-30. In particular, these reviews contain a discussion of the Eskimo division of objects and beings into two seasonal categories and the cultural injunction to avoid mixing elements of the two categories. This is further elaborated in chapter 4 of *Seasonal Variations* and can be readily recognized as one of the earliest sources for later anthropological investigation of categories and their confusion. See, for example, Mary Douglas, *Purity and Danger*, Routledge & Kegan Paul, London, 1966.

23 These references to archaeological data in which Beuchat had a special interest tend to confirm the impression that his collaboration was particularly concentrated on this chapter of the essay.

24 As in so much of Mauss's early work, the influence of Henri Hubert, who co-authored two major essays with him, deserves recognition. In this case, as Mauss himself notes, Hubert's essay, 'Étude sommaire de la représentation du temps dans la religion et la magie', was of particular importance in the shaping of his concluding argument.

25 Oscar Jaszi, 'An Inductive Vindication of Historical Materialism' first published in *Huszadik Szazad*, Budapest, 1906, and reprinted in *The Review: a Quarterly of Pluralist Socialism* (Brussels), vol. 5, 1963, p. 65.

26 Claude Dubar, 'Retour aux textes' in *L'Arc 48: Marcel Mauss*, p. 25.

27 Mary Douglas, 'Symbolic Orders in the Use of Domestic Space' in P. J. Ucko, R. Tringham and G. W. Dimbleby, eds, *Man, Settlement and Urbanism*, Duckworth, London, 1972, pp. 513-14.

28 See, in particular, S. Lukes, *Émile Durkheim*, pp. 226-36.

29 In the introduction to the translation of Hertz, Evans-Pritchard writes: 'If a personal note be allowed, I would, though with serious reservations, identify myself with the *Année* school if a choice had to be made and an intellectual allegiance to be declared'; *Death and the Right Hand*, p. 24.

30 See G. Lienhardt, *Social Anthropology*, Oxford University Press, 1964, pp. 44-51.

31 E. E. Evans-Pritchard, *The Nuer*, Clarendon Press, Oxford, 1940, p. 93.

32 See *Annual Report of the Board of Regents of the Smithsonian*

Institution to July 1895, Washington, 1896, pp. 625 ff.
33 There are two accounts of events surrounding the wreck of the
   Karluk. The first is an appendix, 'The Story of the *Karluk*', written
   mainly by John Hadley and included in V. Stefánsson's *The Friendly
   Arctic*, Macmillan, London, 1921, pp. 704–30; the second is *The Last
   Voyage of the 'Karluk'* as told by her captain, R. A. Bartlett, to
   R. T. Hale, Boston, 1916. This volume contains a group photograph
   (facing p. 10) of members of the expedition, including Beuchat,
   taken just before their departure from Nome.
34 Mauss, *Oeuvres*, vol. III, p. 489.

Introduction

1 Reprinted from *L'Année sociologique*, vol. 9, 1904–5, pp. 39–132.
2 See Durkheim (1899a) and section VI of the *Année sociologique*,
  vols 1-9.
3 We are using the term 'population' for want of a better one. It would
  be quite inaccurate to speak of an Eskimo nation, for the Eskimo
  tribes, themselves poorly defined, have never provided even the
  embryo for such a group. But it would be equally inaccurate to
  imagine that the differences among the tribes of this group are of the
  order of those that distinguish tribes of other so-called primitive
  populations. (The number of Eskimo has been estimated at scarcely
  60,000; see Rink (1887, pp. 31 ff.), whose figures have not been
  disputed by later research.) The entire culture and race show a
  remarkable uniformity. On the unity of the race, see Rink (1887, pp.
  8 ff.) and Bahnson (1892, p. 223). On the unity of the language, see
  Rink (1887, pp. 8 ff.; 1891, pp. 6 ff.) (though we would naturally
  not accept all his hypotheses) and, especially, Thalbitzer (1904, pp.
  225 ff.). This unity was a fact well recognized by the earliest
  explorers and served as the basis of the instructions to Franklin and
  his successors. See Franklin (1823, p. 43), Miertsching (1864, pp. 37,
  42) and Markham (1875, p. 151). On the unity of material culture
  and moral life, see Murdoch (1892), which is full of information.
  The book by Steensby (1905) is especially devoted to material culture
  and constitutes an excellent demonstration of the point we are now
  making. A certain number of specialized ethnographic works are all
  just as convincing. They are Mason (1896a), Murdoch (1885, pp.
  307-16) and Murdoch, 'The forms of the Eskimo bows', *Naturalist*,
  8, p. 869. [This non-existent reference involves a double confusion.
  Murdoch (1892, p. 199) refers to Emil Bessels's observation of a
  bow made from pieces of antlers spliced together. Unfortunately, in
  his footnote, Murdoch mistakenly identifies his source as vol. 8 of
  the *Naturalist* rather than vol. 18 of the *American Naturalist*. Mauss
  copies this directly, attributes the source to Murdoch rather than to
  Bessels and thereby creates this spurious reference. JJF.] On legends,
  see Boas and Rink (1889), Boas (1901, pp. 355 ff.) and Boas (1904).
  The different groups of Eskimo have a single mythology, a single

technology, a single form of social organization and a single language. As far as language is concerned, there are only dialect differences and, in the rest of their collective culture, there are only variations in practice. The present work will also serve to demonstrate that the Eskimo possess only one morphology. It is thus much easier to make sounder comparisons and generalizations.

4 See chapter 1.

5 We cannot list these tribes and their names here. We consider it sufficient to indicate the principal works that deal with this question of geographical nomenclature. Beginning in Alaska, they are the following: Dall (1870, pp. 180 ff.; 1877, pp. 1-8), Porter, (1893), Wells and Kelly (1890), Petitot (1876, pp. xiii ff.) and Boas (1888, pp. 414 ff.). As we shall see (pp. 25, 26), the various groups in Labrador and Greenland do not seem to have tribal names. The map with the best and clearest list is that in Thalbitzer (1904).

6 The founder of this discipline was Friedrich Ratzel, whose principal works, *Anthropogeographie* (vol. 1, 2nd ed., 1899; vol. 2, 1st ed., 1891) and *Politische Geographie* (1897), were reviewed in the *Année sociologique* along with other works of the same kind. See *Année sociologique*, vol. 2, 1899, pp. 522 ff.; vol. 3, 1900, pp. 550 ff.; vol. 4, 1901, pp. 565 ff.; vol. 6, 1903, pp. 539 ff.; vol. 8, 1905, pp. 613, 621. For a résumé by Ratzel, see *Année sociologique*, vol. 3, 1900, pp. 1-14. An exhaustive bibliography of these works up until 1899 can be found in Ratzel (1899, pp. 579 ff.); a continuation of this bibliography can be found listed under 'Géographie humaine' in the *Bibliographie des Annales de Géographie*. The most important recent works of this school are those of the French school of Paul Vidal de la Blache, Emmanuel de Martonne, Jean Brunhes and Albert Demangeon; see Vidal de la Blache (1903a).

7 Naturally, in any account as short as this, we cannot consider works of a kind that, though poorly classified, come closer to sociology than geography because they are, on the whole, studies of historical geography and consist of considerations on the geographical philosophy of social history. These include Ramsay (1902), Mackinder (1904) and, especially, Vidal de la Blache (1903b); see also Vacher (1903). Neither are we going to consider certain sketches, mainly by American ethnographers, that relate even more closely to what we are attempting here. These have mainly to do with the attempt to show the immediate effect of the physical environment on social life, especially in its technological and religious aspects; see particularly McGee (1896), Mason (1896b), Powell (1896), Hubbard (1896) and Fewkes (1896).

8 A later geographer of this school and the only one who really takes exception to this practice is Albert Demangeon. He believes, in fact (1905, pp. 455-6), that land has its effects on man through the mediation of society. He thus arrives at our theory; or rather, we have fixed upon a theory of his which he does not consistently apply. A comparison may help to make the point. W. M. Davis, in a curious article (1903, pp. 413-23), proposes that geography should

account for the human life which the earth supports. Using an interesting schema, he attempts to show lines of correlation that geography has to lay out and the planes these lines transverse. In our opinion, one of these planes is, precisely and always, society; and it is in transversing society that geographical conditions have an effect, via the social mass, on the individual.

9 This is the plan of vol. 1 of Ratzel's *Anthropogeographie*, which is the more sociological of the two volumes. See Ratzel's own résumé (1900).

10 Thus the increase of the population in Meurthe-et-Moselle is the result not only of the existence of mines and canals, etc., but also of the discovery of the treatment process for iron pyrites and of protectionism.

11 For a better understanding of our point of view, an entire critique of these recent works would naturally be necessary. In our opinion, the effects of morphological phenomena are not limited to certain legal phenomena, of the kind, for example, that Brunhes has noted in regard to the regulation of water and irrigation rights; they extend as well to higher spheres of social physiology; see Durkheim (1902, pp. 252 ff.), Durkheim and Mauss (1903) and Bouglé (1903, pp. 75 ff.). Furthermore, it is by means of physiological phenomena, or because of the absence of these phenomena, that land factors produce their effect. Thus when one connects nomadism with the steppe, as Martonne does (1897), one forgets that the Nilotic steppe is, in part, cultivable and it is the absence of agricultural techniques that keeps certain people in a state of nomadism.

12 Steensby (1905) and Riedel (1902). Riedel's work is his inaugural dissertation at Halle.

13 Hassert's study (1895) deals mainly with the Asian origin of the Eskimo and questions of adaptation to the land. Hassert (1902) is a restatement of this first study. See also Boas (1883), Wächter (1898) and Isachsen (1903). To his credit, Captain Isachsen has put forward and demonstrated by his exploration of Devon Island the most probable hypothesis for the settlement of western Greenland; see also Sverdrup (1903, vol. 2, p. 275; English trans. 1904, vol. 2, p. 212). See Faustini (1903, p. 28), and the anonymous review ['The Eskimo exodus'] in the *Geographical Journal*, vol. 23, 1904, p. 392. Faustini divides the Eskimo, on plausible grounds, into two branches: the one in the south-west and the other in the north, who were separated in the area around Nome, Alaska.

14 Mason (1896a).

15 It is useful to provide here a summary bibliography of the principal works that we have used so that they can henceforth be cited in abbreviated form. The most complete and nearly exhaustive bibliographies are to be found in Pilling (1887) and Steensby (1905, pp. 207 ff.).

The oldest works on Greenland are some of the best; among others, there is H. P. Egede (1741). We have also consulted the first edition, Egede (1729); a good French translation is that by Des

Roches de Parthenay (Egede, 1763). Another valuable old work is Cranz (1765). The only good edition, the English one, which is less rare, is Cranz (1767), which deals with the southernmost tribes and constitutes a relatively independent source. Next come the books by H. J. Rink which, besides those already cited, are (1857; 1866–71, English trans., Rink, 1875). All these works deal with the Eskimo of western Greenland. The principal work devoted to the eastern Eskimo is that by Holm (1888). The collection of publications *Meddelelser om Grønland* of the Kommissionen for Ledelsen af de geologiske og geografiske Undersøgelser i Grønland is most valuable. The Commission has kindly sent us a copy, for which we are grateful.

On the Eskimo of Labrador, we have only scattered sources that are not worth citing here; the only monograph that deals with those Eskimo on the southern part of Hudson Bay is Turner (1894).

On the central Eskimo, the better documents are, in order of date, Parry (1824) and Lyon (1824). These two accounts deal with the tribe that settled at Iglulik during two successive winters. Next come the documents by Hall (1864; 1879) which unfortunately must be treated with caution and are, in part, badly produced; those of the Schwatka expedition, mainly the account by Klutschak (1881a), and finally the two monographs by Boas (1888; 1901).

On the Eskimo of the Mackenzie region, we have only scattered information and two unreliable works by Petitot (1876; 1887).

Publications again become abundant when we arrive in Alaska. But the better ones and the only ones that we have consistently used are Murdoch (1892) and Nelson (1899).

Other publications will be cited in the course of this study. Although it may not be possible to claim, as it has been, that the Eskimo constitute one of the best known peoples of the world, we must admit that we have at our command a collection of monographs about them that is relatively satisfactory.

Chapter 1   General morphology

1 A great deal of information on the general morphology of each separate tribal group can be found in Steensby (1905, pp. 50 ff.).

2 On the extent of Eskimo culture in former times, see Steensby (1905, pp. 23 ff. and pp. 50 ff.). The northernmost point which has been found to have been inhabited is at 83°, near Lake Hazeu on the Grinnell Peninsula; see Greely (1886, vol. 1, pp. 379–83). The entire northern archipelago was populated. There is a list of former Eskimo sites that were verified by voyagers prior to 1875 in C. R. Markham (1875, pp. 140 ff.). In the south the extreme point attained was Newfoundland and New Brunswick. Eskimo regularly spent the summer in Newfoundland in the eighteenth century; see Cartwright (1792, vol. 3, pp. 301–13), Packard (1891, p. 245) and Cranz (1770, pp. 301–13). On the other hand, the entire southern

part of Hudson Bay appears to have been equally populated by Eskimo. See Dobbs (1744, p. 49). On the Pacific, they probably occupied the American coast to the Stikine River; see Dall (1877, p. 21). It is particularly remarkable that this immensely extended area which the Eskimo once inhabited was also exclusively a coastal region.

3 On the Itah tribe, see Kane (1856), Hayes (1860; 1867), Bessels (1879), Peary (1898) and Kroeber (1899). (Davis's edition of notes from Hall's journal is worthless.) The recently arrived book by Rasmussen (1905) contributes a considerable amount of new material.

4 Turner (1894, p. 176).

5 Kodiak Island. We consider the Aleuts to be a very distant branch of Eskimo culture and we have, therefore, not taken them into account. Similarly, we consider the Kaniagmiuts, the inhabitants of Kodiak Island, as a mixed group; see Pinart (1873, pp. 12 ff.).

6 On the Yuit or Yuin of East Cape, Siberia, often mistakenly confused with the Chukchi of the Chukchi Peninsula, see Nordenskiöld (1883, vol. 2, pp. 22 ff.) and Krause (1882).

7 Nowhere is there a good list of these tribes, but it is possible to construct one using the descriptions by Porter and his census-takers, Schultze and Woolfe; see Porter (1893, pp. 99-152, 166 ff.). The tribe of Kopagmiut that Petroff (1884, p. 121) describes as inhabiting the interior between Kotzebue Sound and Colville Bar is a pure fabrication; see also Murdoch (1892, p. 47, n. 7) and Steensby (1905, p. 120). The muddle may be explained by the fact that the Kowagmiut were confused with the Nunatagmiut, a mixed tribe that had, in fact, recently succeeded in extending their voyages from the north coast of Kotzebue Sound to the shores of the Arctic Ocean. On the Nooatakamiut (people of the forested land), see Wells and Kelly (1890, p. 14 and the map).

8 The inhabitants of the Asian coast of the Arctic Ocean are in fact tundra-dwellers.

9 One of the best descriptions of Greenland is still that of the elder [H.P.] Egede (1741, pp. 1 ff.), Dalager (1758) and, above all, Kornerup (1880, p. 87).

10 Boas (1888, pp. 414 ff.).

11 Stearns (1884, pp. 22 ff.).

12 The best description is the most recent; see Hanbury (1904, pp. 64 ff.). See also *Geographical Survey of Canada*, 1898. The earlier expeditions of Sir John Richardson, John Rae, P. W. Dease and Thomas Simpson were all made by canoe, and the coast was not visible except at a distance or at landing-points.

13 For a good description of the coast of Alaska, see also Beechey (1831) and the *United States Coast and Geodetic Survey*, 1901.

14 Among others, Ratzel (1899, vol. 1, p. 286). [One possible passage in Ratzel which Mauss may be paraphrasing is the following: '. . . dann ist sie [die Küste] der Uebergang vom Meer zum Land; und endlich ist sie der Uebergang vom Land zum Meer.' JJF.]

15 It is true that Ratzel elsewhere defines the Eskimo as *'Randvölker'*, people on the shore of the 'Oekumene' (1899, vol. 1, pp. 35, 37 ff.). [Mauss is probably referring here to Ratzel (1891, vol. 2, pp. 3-86). JJF.] But this idea, which he develops further, is purely descriptive. In any case, it does not at all explain what it pretends to explain, namely the enormous spread and low density of the Eskimo population.

16 Naturally, this does not apply to Greenland, whose interior is covered by an immense glacier, nor to the entire Arctic archipelago which is populated only by Eskimo.

17 The only areas where regular contact was established between Eskimo and Indians are (1) the mouth of the Mackenzie and (2) the upper Yukon. On the Mackenzie, see Anderson, *Rupert Land*, 1831 [identification uncertain, possibly Anderson, 1856 or 1857. JJF.], Franklin (1823, pp. 48 ff.) and Petitot (1887, pp. 34, 37 ff.). One ought to point out as well that the main reason for these exchanges and gatherings was to trade with whites. On the Yukon, see Porter (1893, p. 123). Again one ought to point out that the tribes of the upper Yukon are under white influence and have become heavily intermingled with the Indians called Ingalik.

18 On the linguistic unity of the Eskimo, see the works cited in the Introduction, n. 3. It is still quite remarkable that for the region whose language is best known, that of western Greenland, one can distinguish only two dialects, a northern and a southern, separated by various significant differences. Thalbitzer (1904, pp. 396 ff.) and Schultz-Lorentzen (1904, pp. 302 ff.) tell us specifically of a former difference which the two populations are aware of but which nas now disappeared. The few contrary comments about the lack of comprehension between distant Eskimo groups are based entirely on casual remarks by ill-informed observers who were unable to spend the time necessary to appreciate the ways in which dialects shade into one another.

19 We refer mainly to the 'Arctic' district of Alaska; see Petroff (1884, section V) and Porter (1893, section VII). The list of tribes given by Dall (1877, pp. 37 ff.) not only differs from that of Petroff (1884, pp. 15 ff., 125 ff.) which contributed to its compilation but also differs completely from Porter's (Woolfe's). And even between Porter and his correspondent there are divergences; see Porter (1893, pp. 62 and 142). Finally, in Wells and Kelly, there is yet another table of divergent dialects which gives their relation to the tribes (1890, pp. 14, 26, 27; see also their excellent map which is clearly only very approximate).

20 The only proper names that we find are place-names. Even when we are not told that these names bear the suffix *-miut*, which designates the inhabitants of a place, such is the case. The affixes that are missing in Rink (1866-71, vol. 1, p. 65) reappear in the English translation (1875, p. 20) without any indication that this usage applies to the inhabitants of the place. Any connection between different 'wintering-places' is moreover said to be non-existent; see Rink (1875, p. 23).

21 Turner (1894, pp. 179 ff.): Itiwynmiut, 'People of the North';
   Koksoagmiut, 'People of the Koksoak River', etc.

22 See the lists of names in Richardson (1851, vol. 1, p. 87; 1861, p. 299).

23 The maps which the Eskimo gave to Parry (1824, Eskimaux Charts I
   and II facing pp. 197-8) show that although there may not be
   borders, there are at least defined areas of winter trekking. See
   especially Boas (1888, pp. 419-60 and his accompanying map which
   we have partially reproduced as Figure 6 in chapter 2). The lists of
   names from Parry and Richardson and those from Boas are identical
   with those in Hall (1864) for Frobisher Bay and Cumberland Sound
   as well as with those that Hall gives for western Baffin Land and
   Hudson Bay.
       For boundaries on Baffin Land, see Boas (1888, pp. 421, 444,
   463). (Nugumiut are considered strangers in Cumberland Sound;
   Padlirmiut do not encroach upon the summer hunting territory of
   the Talirpingmiut nor those of the Kingnamiut.) The maps of these
   boundaries provided by Boas should not, however, be interpreted in
   a conventional sense, especially since they indicate areas of travel in
   the interior as if they were genuine areas of settlement. On the
   boundaries of Melville Peninsula, Hudson Bay and the Back River,
   we have a collection of statements from Richardson (1851, vol. 2, p.
   128), Schwatka in Gilder (1881, pp. 38 ff.) and Klutschak (1881a,
   pp. 66, 68; 1881b, pp. 418 ff.). See, however, Boas (1888, p. 466),
   who disagrees with Klutschak.

24 As far as Alaska is concerned, there is no unanimity even among the
   small group of observers who went through the Bering Strait
   between 1880 and 1890. Compare the list of names in Petroff (1884,
   p. 15) with those in Porter (1893, p. 164) or Nelson (1899, pp. 13 ff.
   plus map); or compare Nelson's list with that of Woolfe, Schanz and
   Porter in Porter (1893, p. 108) or that of Jacobsen (1884, pp.
   166 ff.).

25 Richardson (1851, vol. 2, p. 128) cites the text by Simpson (1875, p.
   238) on the hunting territories reserved for families at Point
   Barrow. Murdoch (1892, p. 27) says he is unable to substantiate this
   fact. [This note is difficult to decipher and I have translated it as it
   stands. Mauss has apparently confused John Simpson (1875) with
   Thomas Simpson (1843). On the page given by Mauss, Richardson
   quotes a letter by John Rae that refers to the explorations of
   Thomas Simpson and P. W. Dease. To complicate matters further,
   Murdoch says nothing about hunting territories on p. 27; but on p.
   267 he refers to Richardson (1851, vol. 1, pp. 244, 351), who
   remarks on the 'hunting grounds of families being kept sacred'.
   JJF.]

26 On the wars in Baffin Land and to the west of Hudson Bay, see
   Kumlien (1879, p. 28). This is different from Boas (1888, pp. 464-5),
   who, however, provides contrary evidence (1901, pp. 18, 27). For
   Alaska, see Wells and Kelly (1890, pp. 13, 14 and the tale of the
   Nunatagmiut, p. 25); see also Petroff (1884, p. 128) and Nelson
   (1899, p. 127).

27 A group in Baffin Land, the Oqomiut, appears indeed to comprise a collection of tribal aggregates; see Boas (1888, p. 424).

28 Rink (1877, vol. 2, p. 250; 1875, pp. 17, 21). Regarding the Tahagmiut, see Turner (1894, p. 177) and Boas (1888, p. 424).

29 See Kane (1856, vol. 2, p. 103).

30 For a definition of the settlement in Greenland, see H. P. Egede (1741, p. 60).

31 There seems to be a kind of regular return of old men to the place of their birth, at least in some cases; see Boas (1888, p. 466). See also the tale from Greenland, no. 36 (Nivnitak) in Rink (1875, p. 247) and the rite in Klutschak (1881a, p. 153).

32 Among the list of places and settlements that we will cite, the best and most scientifically established is that for western Greenland; see Thalbitzer (1904, p. 333). It is worth noting that almost all the names designate specific natural objects. Thus the name by which Eskimo designate themselves is nothing more than a geographical one.

33 See the tables in Petroff (1884, pp. 12 ff.) and Porter (1893, pp. 18 ff.). On these lists of names, see the works already cited in n. 19 above.

34 In the present state of our knowledge, we face an insoluble difficulty in knowing whether an individual is designated by the place where he was born or where he lives. We are told that on very solemn occasions (the festivities that we will discuss later, see p. 68) an individual states his name and place of birth. See Boas (1888, p. 605; 1901, pp. 142 ff.); for more or less the same custom, see Nelson (1899, p. 373).

35 For a particularly good example from Greenland, see Rink (1875, p. 23).

36 Rink (1875, p. 256).

37 For a good description of the rights of two villages over their hinterland, see Murdoch (1892, pp. 27 ff.).

38 Hall (1864, vol. 1, p. 320; vol. 2, pp. 24, 34).

39 See Turner (1894, p. 201) and Boas (1888, p. 61). It appears that this taboo lasts only until a newborn child takes his name; see Cranz (1770, p. 110, note).

40 Boas (1888, p. 613) and Nelson (1899, p. 291). We are told, more precisely (Nelson, 1899, p. 289), that among the Malemiut, the name is conferred in the winter settlement; a child receives a temporary name on the tundra where his parents are hunting. To interpret the extent and significance of this custom in all Eskimo societies would require an extensive study, but for the moment we can say that this system of perpetual reincarnation gives the Eskimo settlement the singular aspect of an American Indian clan.

41 For examples of this relative permeability, in connection with the Iglulik, see Parry (1824, pp. 124 ff.).

42 Graah (1832, pp. 118 ff.).

43 Graah, who made his voyage during the summer, found about 600 inhabitants living in an unknown number (17 + x) of settlements.

Along almost twice the length of coastline, Holm found no more
than 182 Eskimo; see Hansen (1888) and Holm (1887-8, pp. 185 ff.).

44 The history of the formation of Frederiksdal can be found in the
Periodical Accounts of the United Brethren, beginning in vol. 2, p.
414: thirty people come back from Lichtenau and 200 non-believers
from the south and east concentrate there, while a large number of
others announce their wish to come; see *Periodical Accounts*, vol. 2,
p. 421. In 1827, 1828 and 1829 the population in the district grows
regularly with additions from the south-east; see *Periodical
Accounts*, vol. 10, pp. 41, 68, 103, 104 and also Holm's account
(1887-8, p. 201) based on Mission archives.

45 Holm (1887-8, p. 201) tells of a man from Sermilik whom he saw at
Angmagssalik and who, as a child, had seen Graah.

46 See Holm (1887-8, pp. 193 ff.).

47 H. P. Egede (1741, p. 101); for Disco, see P. H. Egede (1788, pp.
235 ff.), and Cranz (1765, vol. 1, pp. 380 ff.) for Godhavn and the
southern settlements. These provide statistical information on the
Danish and southern Missions which Dalager (1758) confirms. But
none of these documents is entirely reliable; they deal only with the
fluid populations associated with the missionaries. The figures in
Rink (1877, vol. 2, pp. 259 ff.) are not of great interest; we are
using only the most recent sources.

48 See Ryberg (1894, pp. 114, 115, 121 and Table G; 1904, p. 172). For
the proportion of men and women at Angmagssalik, see the texts
cited above.

49 See Hansen (1888, pp. 204 ff.) and Ryder (1895a, p. 144).

50 On these various fluctuations and their specific causes, see Ryberg
(1894, pp. 120, 122). An analysis of the various statistics contained
in the *Periodical Accounts* of the Moravian Brethren since 1774
would show that the same thing regularly happens in Labrador. In
Boas (1888, pp. 425 ff.) there is a series of statistical data on the
Oqomiut, their four subtribes and their eight settlements, as well as
their age, sex and status. These data are remarkably similar to those
from Greenland. The tables from Captain Comer and the Reverend
Mr Peck on the Kinipetu and Aivillirmiut fit the same pattern; see
Boas (1901, p. 7).

51 Wrangell (1839, pp. 141 ff.). The advantage of Glasunov's journey
is that it was carried out in winter, and it retains this advantage over
later censuses. Petroff (1884, pp. 23 ff.) summarizes the
inadequacies of Russian censuses before 1870.

52 Petroff (1884, pp. 4, 17 ff.).

53 See Appendix 1.

54 Porter gives a detailed description of the various settlements, each
described in turn with a certain amount of information on winter
settlements and summer ones (1893, pp. 100-14, 154, 170).

55 See Petroff (1884, p. 12) and Porter (1893, p. 5). Kassiachamiut had
50 inhabitants (1893, p. 164).

56 Petroff (1884) reports that ninety-six Europeans lived in the same
district.

57 For the islands, see Porter (1893, pp. 110 ff.) and Nelson (1899, pp. 6 and 256). King Island and Nunivak had 400 inhabitants each.

58 Porter (1893, p. 162).

59 We are not considering, and thus not discussing, cases that fall far below this mean, as for example, the 'single house' or the 'summer camp'; see Porter (1893, p. 165) and Petroff (1884, pp. 11-12).

60 See Porter (1893, p. 137).

61 This is one of the earliest reported facts about the Eskimo. It is to be found even in Vormius, *Museum Naturale*, Copenhagen, 1618, p. 15. [This is apparently a reference to a work by the naturalist Ole Worm, 1588-1654; but the specific work that Mauss has in mind is uncertain. JJF.] For later sources, see Coats (1852, p. 35) and H. P. Egede (1741, p. 60). See also the first edition of this volume (1729, p. 27); it is so evident that there is perhaps no author who has not reported it. It is even said that Eskimo women completely refuse to believe that European women are able to have ten and twelve children. See Woolfe in Porter (1893, p. 137) – the maximum appears to be four to five children. The only contrary case on which we have figures is that of a Kinipetu family with eight children recorded by Captain Comer in 1898 (Boas, 1901, pp. 6-7) but this is probably an observational error. (The same author mentions two families of that size, but only one appears in his table.)

62 In Appendix 2 we publish data taken from Porter. For the number of widows, the census documents on the Aivilik are in agreement: six widows (?) among thirty-four women. By contrast, there are only two widows among the Kinipetu, but this results from a larger number of polygamous marriages.

63 See C. R. Markham (1875, pp. 163 ff.), Peary (1898, vol. 1, preface, p. vii, appendix I) and Sverdrup (1903, vol. 1, preface; 1904, vol. 1, preface). Given the animal resources, these authors reasonably contend that *small* expeditions, even with poor provisions, have a better chance of surviving than better provisioned expeditions that are too large. Later expeditions from North America, D. T. Hanbury's in particular, like the early expeditions by Franz Boas, C. F. Hall and Frederick Schwatka, were made by travellers who joined Eskimo groups. Franklin's well-known fate was precisely because he had too many men with him. The first person to recognize this law was probably Hall (1864, vol. 1, p. xii).

64 The recent introduction of domesticated reindeer to Alaska is probably going to change the very morphology of Eskimo societies that succeed in rearing them; see Sheldon, *Report on the Introduction of Reindeer in Alaska*, Rep. USNM, 1894. [Sheldon's paper is not in this Report. The precise reference is uncertain. JJF.]

65 See Hall (1864, vol. 1, p. 138) and Peary (1898, vol. 2, p. 15).

66 Although hunting takes place twice each year at Point Barrow – a place where whales periodically pass from the Arctic Ocean to the Pacific and back again – it is becoming less and less productive; see Murdoch (1892, p. 272) and Woolfe in Porter (1893, p. 145).

European whalers have shifted their most important fisheries to the mouths of the Mackenzie River.

67 For an excellent description of the general conditions of Eskimo life, see Boas (1888, pp. 419-20).

68 On the closure of the seas in the North American archipelago, see C. R. Markham (1875, pp. 62 ff.) or the *Arctic Pilot*, 1904, vol. 1, pp. 28 ff.

69 On the causes of the depopulations of the northern archipelago, see Sverdrup (1903, vol. 1, p. 145).

70 On the climatic, maritime and economic conditions of life, see Holm (1887-8, pp. 287 ff.; 1888, pp. 47-8) Ryder, (1895a, pp. 138 ff.) and Ryberg (1894, pp. 144 ff.). We might add that before the arrival of Holm, the situation at Angmagssalik was grave as a result of the almost complete loss of dogs (1887-8, p. 134). In Table 1, we can see that in favourable years there is a simple movement of the population.

71 Nansen (1903, pp. 46 ff.).

72 Conditions of existence are equally precarious in Baffin Land and, in recent years, famine has regularly reduced the population. For the history of certain tribes, see Boas (1888, pp. 426 ff.).

73 The picture we sketch of life at Point Barrow is based on Simpson (1875, p. 245 (reproduced from *Parliamentary Reports*, 1855)) and Murdoch (1892, pp. 45 ff.).

74 The statement by Woolfe in Porter (1893, p. 145) that the proportion of births was reduced from five to one merits only relative credence. Petroff's documents (1884, p. 14) are completely incorrect; in fact, there is not even an enumeration of villages.

75 Moreover, the group intervenes forcibly, as a group, to limit the number of members in its charge: (1) by infanticide, especially of female children, as is evident for numerous tribes; (2) by murder of weak and sickly children which is also generally reported; (3) by abandonment of the sick and elderly and (4) by abandonment of widows, thus leaving them to die, as is reported in some tribes. On infanticide, see H. P. Egede (1741, p. 91), Cranz (1765, III, 3, 21), Rasmussen (1905, p. 29; dealing with the tribe at Cape York), Boas (1888, p. 580), Bessels (1884, p. 874; 1879, p. 185 on the infanticide of children of both sexes at Itah), Gilder (1881, pp. 246-7), Murdoch (1892, p. 417), Simpson (1875, p. 250) and Nelson (1899, p. 289). The purpose of infanticide is evidently to reduce the number of non-hunters. On widow abandonment, see Parry (1824, pp. 400, 409, 529), Lyon (1824, p. 323) and Hall (1864, vol. 1, p. 97).

Chapter 2   Seasonal morphology

1 Frobisher (1867, p. 283), Hakluyt (1589, p. 628), Hall in Fox (1635, p. 56), Coats (1852, pp. 35, 75, 89, 90), H. P. Egede (1729, p. 27; 1741, p. 60), Cranz (1765, III, 1, 4) and Dalager (1758). We do not give other early authors, all of whom were acquainted with the

sources we have just cited. The book by Cranz, in particular, was extremely popular and was used by all travellers and ethnographers.

2 On the Eskimo tent in general, see Murdoch (1892, p. 84).

3 For this word, see the dictionaries: P. H. Egede (1750, p. 128), Parry (1824, p. 562), Erdmann (1864) and Wells and Kelly (1890, pp. 36, 43). See also Rink (1891, pp. 72 ff.).

4 See Steensby (1905, p. 143) who arrived at the same conclusion as we have. The cone is, in some cases, sectioned in front where it forms a perfect cone. The perfect cone form is typical of western Eskimo culture. Early Greenland reports show the tent with a kind of doorway; see the plates in H. P. Egede (1741, p. 61), Cranz (1765, vol. 1, plate III) and Graah (1832, plate VI facing p. 73). This is probably an artistic exaggeration that transforms the perpendicular curtain of skin, which hangs down and closes the front of the tent, into a door.

5 Coats (1852, p. 35) notes the difference between Eskimo dwellings and Indian (Cree and Montagnais) tents. See Hearne (1795, p. 180).

6 Holm (1888, pp. 71 ff., plates X and XI) and Graah (1832, p. 73).

7 Holm (1888, pp. 72, 74).

8 See the good descriptions by Parry and Lyon in Parry (1824, pp. 270 ff., plate facing p. 271). The structure was even then often constructed of narwhal bones. On his first voyage to the north of Baffin Land, Parry had seen another kind of tent which utilized whale-ribs, probably because of the lack of wood (1821, p. 283).

9 Boas (1888, p. 552) and Chappell (1817, p. 29). For the types of tent in Alaska, see Nelson (1899, p. 258 ff.). For the southernmost abandoned sites found by Hall's expeditions, see Bessels (1879, p. 235). For others, see A. H. Markham (1874, p. 285; 1878, pp. 79, 391) and Greely (1886, p. 47, n. 2). Those found by Sverdrup (1903, pp. 121, 171) all consisted of circles of round stones which suggest tents of the regular type. Only one abandoned site, seen by Lyon once at Cape Montague, cannot be explained as the remains of a tent; see Parry (1824, p. 62). The houses on the islands of the Bering Strait are a genuine exception to this rule; see Nelson (1899, pp. 255-6). But the conditions of Eskimo life on these islands, where they live virtually settled on true escarpments, are specific enough to explain the exception. Nevertheless isolated summer houses appear to be often seen in Alaska; see Nelson (1899, pp. 260 ff.) and Jacobsen (1884, p. 161).

10 For Angmagssalik, see Holm (1888, p. 87); for western Greenland, Rink (1875, p. 19) and H. P. Egede (1741, p. 60); for the central Eskimo, Boas (1888, p. 581); Klutschak (1881a) and Schwatka (1885) among the Netchillik and Ukusiksalik, Hall (1864; 1879) among the Nugumiut (on his first voyage) and among the Aiwillik (on his second), and Hanbury (1904) between the Back River and the Mackenzie; all made their *summer* explorations with Eskimo families by living in their tents, or, depending on the time of the year, in their snow igloos; see Petitot (1876, p. xx), Murdoch

(1892, pp. 80 ff.) and Nelson (1899, pp. 260 ff.). From lists cited in Table 1, it is possible to deduce that each family in eastern Greenland has its own tent. Furthermore, it seems impossible that a tent would hold more than one or two families and, from this viewpoint, we believe that the statement by Back (1836, p. 383) that he found thirty-five people in three tents among the Ukusiksalik is inaccurate.

11 See Lyon in Parry (1824, pp. 270, 360).

12 Graah (1832, p. 93), however, describes a double tent with a partition.

13 The house is called an *iglu*. On this word, see the dictionaries cited above in note 3 of this chapter and Rink (1891, pp. 72 ff.). Exceptions are not at all convincing. If there are different names, or even if an equivalent word has more or less the same sense, this is for specific reasons. Thus in Alaska there is another word for the apartment; see Wells and Kelly (1890, p. 44). We will see why, in the central regions, the word *iglu* has been restricted to the snow-house, the house itself being limited to this one type of dwelling.

14 For the following discussion, see Steensby (1905, pp. 182 ff.), with whom we agree on the most important point, that of understanding the primitive character of the long-house. The effort by Steensby to link the Eskimo winter house to the Indian long-house (with Mandan and Iroquois houses as examples) shows, however inappropriate this may be, that for this author as for us, these two types of house are homologous.

15 The Mandan house, for example, lacks both passage and bench; nevertheless Steensby wants to compare it with the Eskimo house. Moreover, it possesses, *like all Indian houses*, a central hearth which occurs only in Eskimo houses in southern Alaska. The winter houses of the north-west coast of America have benches and partitions; see Niblack (1890, pp. 95 ff.). But the presence of a central hearth and the absence of the passage negates all parallels.

16 Holm (1888, pp. 66-7). For south-east Greenland in former times, see Graah (1832, p. 32 and plate II, which is excellent). See also Nansen (1903, p. 67) and S. Rink (1900, p. 43).

17 In fact, H. P. Egede expressly mentions that, in time of sexual licence, couples lie in the empty area under the platform. On the house, see H. P. Egede (1741, plate IX, facing p. 61) and Cranz (1765, plate IV). On this custom, see H. P. Egede (1729, p. 36) and P. H. Egede (1750, p. 100 under the entry *malliserpok*). On the other hand, it is indeed remarkable that the Angmagssalik house corresponds so well, especially in the form of its roof, with early authors' reproductions of western Greenland houses and so poorly with recent authors' depictions as well as some early ones for this region; see Davis in Hakluyt (1589, p. 788). See especially the woodcuts in Rink (1875, pp. 105, 191, 223); also the Danish edition (1866-71) and the Eskimo edition (1860) in which plates 3 and 4 are better. The house with upright walls, relatively clear of the earth

and covered with a roof supported on beams placed on the walls, gives the distinct impression of a European house and was perhaps built under old Norse influence. On this influence see Tylor (1883-4, pp. 275 ff.). Not all of Tylor's comparisons, however, appear to be well founded.

18 Only here does the edge of the bench extend to the floor leaving no empty space; see Figures 3 and 4.

19 Here the bench once more is raised with empty space below; see Murdoch (1892, fig. 11) and Nelson (1899, figs 80 ff.).

20 See H. P. Egede (1741, p. 63). Cranz (1765, III, 1, 4) is even more precise on the placement of the lamp. The partitioning of the bench normally disappears where there are proper compartments and, in short, is probably restricted to Greenland. In western Greenland the Eskimo lamp was not replaced by the European stove, except among the rich.

21 See the texts cited in the previous note plus Graah (1832, p. 35) and S. Rink (1900, p. 29, note 1).

22 For the houses of the Mackenzie region and the Anderson, see especially Petitot (1876, p. xxi and plate; 1887, pp. 41, 49, 50). If this passage were made of pieces of ice among the Kragmalivit (*sic*), there is a contradiction between the statements and the design based on the sketch (?) on p. 193. See Franklin (1828, pp. 41, 121 and plate); for Point Atkinson, see Richardson in Franklin (1828, pp. 215-16). The plan and the section by section plan lack two supporting beams for the central rectangle. See the information in Miertsching (1864, pp. 35, 37), Hooper (1853, p. 243) and Richardson (1851, vol. 1, p. 30; 1861, pp. 330 ff.). The description by Schultz (1895, p. 122) is based neither on observation nor on the statements by Bompas and Sainville, and is nothing but a repetition of H. P. Egede or Cranz.

23 See Petitot (1887, p. 41).

24 Richardson in Franklin (1828, pp. 216 ff.). The passage, based on plate 8, seems to be too short.

25 For the house at Point Barrow, see Murdoch (1892, pp. 72 ff.) and Simpson (1875, pp. 256, 258). For the house at Bering Strait, see Nelson (1899, pp. 253 ff., figs 80 ff.).

26 For the plan of the house at Cape Nome, see Nelson (1899, p. 254).

27 See Nelson (1899, fig. 74) and Elliott (1886, pp. 378-9). To the south, in the Nushagak district, the central wooden fireplace which is often used affects the construction of the house and tends to make the Eskimo house more like that of the Chilcotin; see Jacobsen (1884, p. 321). On the various types of house in Alaska, see Porter (1893, pp. 146 ff. and figs on pp. 96, 106). Reports from early expeditions by Beechey (1831, vol. 2, pp. 568-9) and by the Russians (Wrangell, 1839, pp. 143 ff.) are in agreement and demonstrate that the distribution of house types is just about the same.

28 For the house made of whale-ribs, see Nelson (1899, pp. 257 ff.)

and Petroff (1884, pp. 38 ff.). For the Siberian Eskimo, see Nelson (1899, p. 263).

29 For these houses, see especially Boas (1888, pp. 548 ff.), Kumlien (1879, p. 43) and Hall (1864, vol. 1, p. 131; vol. 2, p. 289). Figures 499-502 in Boas (1888) are particularly interesting (fig. 500 is taken from Kumlien), as they explain the nature of the abandoned sites found by Parry (1824, p. 105), which are evidently the remains of *qarmang*. Hall expressly mentions the fact that the Nugumiut gave up this mode of construction and made snow igloos only because they no longer had whale-ribs. See also Markham (1874, pp. 263-4).

30 For the houses of this region, see Parry (1824, p. 280; for the ruins on the Iglulik plateau, pp. 258, 358, 545), Lyon (1824, p. 115) and Boas (1901, p. 96).

31 Parry expressly mentions the absence of driftwood and the ensuing construction problems. Boas also mentions that the house made of whale-ribs was replaced by the igloo. On the winter houses at the abandoned sites on Bathurst Island, see Boas (1883, p. 128) and Ross (1835, p. 389). The whale-rib houses are mentioned in the traditions of Greenland, and indeed documented; see Carstensen (1890, p. 124).

32 It may appear that the igloo is a very primitive feature of Eskimo culture, for we know that the temporary snow shelter is used everywhere and the snow-cutting knife was part of prehistoric Eskimo material culture. But there are igloos and igloos, and in our opinion the permanent snow igloo, used as a winter house, is of recent origin. The igloo with a passage is unknown except where we have indicated; see H. P. Egede (1741, illustration on p. 71) and Rink (1875, fig. on p. 247). The Eskimo at Smith Strait expressly told Rasmussen that immigrants from Baffin Land had taught them how to make a proper igloo; see Rasmussen (1905, p. 31).

33 Boas (1888, pp. 539 ff., 1901, pp. 95 ff., fig. 40 on p. 97), Hall (1864, vol. 1, p. 21) and Kumlien (1879, fig. 26 on p. 40).

34 See Parry (1824, pp. 159, 160 and plate facing, pp. 358, 499 and p. 500, which shows an excellent plan of a composite igloo). The best plan is provided by Augustus from the tribe at Fort Churchill; see Franklin (1828, p. 287). See also Lewis (1904, pp. 47, 55, 56, and 94 with photograph, 'Little Whale R.'), Tyrrell (1898, pp. 136-7, p. 179, with a plan which relates to Labrador and the region of Chesterfield Fiord), Hanbury (1904, pp. 77-8, with plan from Baker Lake), Gilder (1881, p. 256), Schwatka (1885, p. 18), Klutschak (1881a, p. 23), Ross (1835, p. 230, for the Netchillirmiut) and Hall (1879, p. 128). If one believes certain less reliable authors, the igloo is supposed to be the form of the winter house in Labrador; see Maclean (1849, vol. 2, pp. 145-6) and Ballantyne (1867, pp. 28 ff.). Apart from the fact that the Ungava igloo has no passage (Turner, 1894, fig. 48), the evidence is restricted to Eskimo from Hudson Strait and Ungava Bay whose culture has rather degenerated; and it is certain that the Greenland

type of house had preceded the igloo even there; see Turner (1894, pp. 224 ff.) and Murdoch (1892, p. 228). For a description of the old Labrador house, see *The Moravians in Labrador*, 1833, p. 17.

35 See the drawings in Boas (1888, pp. 546 ff.; 1901, p. 96).

36 See Parry (1824, p. 502).

37 See Frobisher (1867, first voyage, pp. 82, 84; second voyage, Cape Warwick, pp. 137-8, describes a village of *qarmang*.)

38 Coats (1852, pp. 35, 76) and Ellis (1748, p. 87). On the ruins on Melville Peninsula, see Bellot (1854, p. 354).

39 It is certain that there were no actual enclosed seas a few centuries ago and that this change was the result of the shift in polar currents; see *Arctic Pilot*, 1905, pp. 11 ff. and Richardson (1861, pp. 210 ff.).

40 See the texts cited above in note 30 and Lyon (1825, p. 67).

41 See Hall (1864, vol. 1).

42 On the morphological changes undergone by this tribe, see Preuss (1899, pp. 38-43).

43 See Ross (1819, vol. 1, pp. 114 ff.), Kane (1856, vol. 1, pp. 206, 416 ff.) and Hayes (1860, p. 224). The change was already apparent in 1861 at the time of Hayes's second expedition (1867, p. 245). Moreover Hans Hendrik, the Greenland Eskimo, had fled among them and it was at this period that there occurred the great immigration which Rasmussen recounts (1905, pp. 21 ff.), and whose significance Peary somehow seems to ignore and Hayes, Hall and Bessels seem to grasp. On the actual situation see Peary (1898, vol. 1, p. xlix and Appendix), Astrup (1898, pp. 138 ff.) and, in particular, infinitely the most reliable book, that of Rasmussen (1905).

44 They carried on only the hunting of bears, birds and reindeer, along with the dangerous hunting at the edge of the ice.

45 The term *umiak* definitely persisted; see Kane (1856, vol. 2, pp. 124 ff.).

46 On these small houses, see especially Peary (1898, vol. 1, pp. 113 ff.), with the house-plans and cross-sections by Astrup (1898, p. 108) from the village of Keate, Northumberland Island. On construction, see Peary (1898, vol. 1, pp. 87, 91) and J. Peary (1893; 1903, p. 67 plus photographs of Itah). See also Rasmussen (1905, pp. 9 ff.). The igloo is now in fact replacing the stone house.

47 See especially Kane (1856, vol. 1, p. 124 and vol. 2, the Itah hut opposite p. 113); the drawing is certainly stylishly done. See also Ross (1819, p. 130).

48 See Ryder (1895b, pp. 290 ff.). The statement that this house has only one place for a lamp (p. 299) and, therefore, contains only one family does not seem justified. See Drygalski (1897, vol. 1, p. 585).

49 See Boas (1883, p. 128) and the texts he cites, also Greely (1886, pp. 379 ff.).

50 See the catalogue of ruins in Markham (1875, pp. 115 ff.).

51 Moreover, all of the northernmost ruins are evidently the remains

of populations who were ready to emigrate or almost on the point of extinction. But in the Neu Herrnhut report of 1757, Cranz (1767, vol. 2, p. 258, note) reports that during a famine on Kangek Island, fifteen people who were unable to light their lamps for lack of oil took refuge in a very small stone house where they were able to warm themselves more easily, particularly by contact with one another. It is reasonable to suppose that similar causes would produce a similar contraction, if not of the winter family, at least of its dwelling.

52 Nearly all the texts cited above have information on this question pertaining to long-houses or composite houses. Suffice it to say that at least two families live or lived in the only small house that was actually inhabited, that at Smith Strait. See Hayes (1860, p. 64), Kane (1856, vol. 2, pp. 114, 116, which contains some improbable elements) and Hayes (1867, pp. 262, 270, where one family goes to settle with more than three others among the Kalutunah at Ittiblik (or Itiblu, according to Peary)). Moreover, the introduction of the igloo has changed the morphology itself.

53 For the maximum attained in Alaska, see Porter (1893, p. 164). Jacobsen describes the house of a rich Malemiut, indeed the chief at Owirognak, in which there are seven groups of relatives including adopted relatives (1884, p. 241).

54 For the maximum attained at Angmagssalik, where the house is mistaken for the winter settlement, see Holm (1888, pp. 87 ff.); see also Table 1.

55 Cranz (1765, III, 1, 4).

56 See Appendix 1. Those Alaskan villages in which the number of families coincides with the number of houses are Indian villages.

57 See the texts cited in n. 34. The description given by Lyon of an Iglulik house showing two Eskimo families on the same bench of the igloo is not quite correct.

58 See the texts cited in n. 25; see also Petitot (1876, p. xxviii).

59 See the plates in Rink (1875, pp. 74, 86, etc). For Labrador, see *Periodical Accounts*, 1790.

60 See Murdoch (1892, p. 83). At Nunivak Island, the house normally has four families. The same is true in the Nushagak district; see Porter (1893, pp. 108, 126). Probably on the basis of this fact, Boas believed he could definitely connect the Eskimo winter house with that of the Indians of the north-west coast (1891).

61 This can, perhaps, be deduced from several indicative descriptions, but it is formally stated and demonstrated in the drawing of the layout of Angmagssalik. See Holm (1888, p. 66 and plate XXIII). Number 7, the old widower, has a place to himself but no lamp.

62 On the *kashim* in general, see Richardson (1851, vol. 1, p. 365; 1861, pp. 318-19).

63 On the *kashim* in Alaska, see Nelson (1899, pp. 241 ff.). The earliest texts expressly mention it; see Glasunov in Wrangell (1839, pp. 145, 149, 151, 154), Beechey (1831, vol. 1, p. 267; vol. 2, pp. 542, 550, 569), Zagoskin in Petroff (1884, pp. 38 ff.) and Simpson

(1875, p. 259 (Point Barrow)). The censuses by Dall (1870, p. 406), Petroff (1884, pp. 35 ff.) and Porter (1893, pp. 103 ff.) are full of information; see also Elliott (1886, pp. 385-6). Prosperous villages have two or three *kashim*; see Nelson (1899, pp. 242 ff., 391), where it is clear that, at Kushunuk on Cape Vancouver, two *kashim* were in use at the same time, and Porter (1893, pp. 105, 107, 114, 115, etc.). Jacobsen tells of a legend about a village at the mouth of the Yukon with one hundred *kashim* (1884, pp. 179, 207); see also Nelson (1899, p. 242). See the other enumerations in Jacobsen (1884, pp. 225, 226, 228) of villages with several *kashim*. It is very difficult to know the kind of social structure to which these two *kashim* correspond and what their use might be. Perhaps they are linked to the clan organization that Nelson noted. The village at Point Barrow which had three *kashim* in 1851 had only two in 1856; see Murdoch (1892, pp. 79 ff.) and Woolfe in Porter (1893, p. 144) (we do not know what to make of the fact that these *kashim* were built of ice in 1889).

64 On the *kashim* at Point Warren, see Miertsching (1864, p. 121), Armstrong (1857, p. 159) and Petitot (1876, p. xxx). For an important description of the *kashim* on Point Atkinson, see Richardson in Franklin (1828, pp. 215-16). See also the texts cited above and Richardson (1851, vol. 1, pp. 254-5).

65 Boas (1888, pp. 601 ff.) and Hall (1879, p. 220). The ruins reported by Parry (1824, pp. 362 ff.) are evidently those of former *kashim* made of whale-ribs. The memory of festivals and practices was preserved. Beechey (1831, vol. 2, p. 542), who took part in Parry's first expedition, compares the *kashim* at Point Hope with that of the eastern Eskimo. For Gore Bay, see Lyon (1824, p. 61). See also Boas (1901, tale 16) about a *kashim* of stone.

66 Okkak's letter, 1791, in *Periodical Accounts*, 1792, vol. 1, p. 86: 'The Kivalek people built a snow house to game and dance in, and being reproved for it, their answer was "that it was so difficult to catch whales, they would have a katche-game to allure them."' But some women who had danced suddenly die and the 'gaming house' is knocked down. It is remarkable that Erdmann's dictionary, which we have at least leafed through, contains no reference to the word '*kache*' (?) '*qagche*' (?). For Ungava Bay, see also Turner, *American Naturalist*, 1887. [Precise reference uncertain. JJF.]

67 On Disco, see Rink (1886, p. 141). See, more precisely, the tale in Thalbitzer (1904, pp. 275, 297).

68 See Rink (1875, p. 8, plus tales on pp. 273-6). See Kleinschmidt (1871, pp. 124-5); Rink (1887, p. 26; 1891, section 20, no. 16, section 29, no. 11). Probable indications, among others, in Cranz (1767, vol. 2, pp. 29, 73: Report on Neu Herrnhut for 1743 and 1744, and pp. 365, 367) suggest the existence of some kind of *kashim*.

69 See Elliott (1886, pp. 385-6) and Jacobsen (1884, p. 321).

70 Boas (1888, pp. 601-2; 1901, p. 141, on the Nugumiut) and Hall (1864, vol. 2, p. 320).

71 See Jacobsen (1884, p. 323).
72 See pp. 57-62 below.
73 Boas (1901, p. 141 on the Nugumiut) and Murdoch (1892, p. 83).
74 Schanz in Porter (1893, p. 102, which appears to be copied from Glasunov) and Nelson (1899, p. 285, etc.).
75 Nelson (1899, p. 287), Jacobsen (1884, p. 212) and Elliott (1886).
76 Besides the *kashim*, the tent and the long-house, there exist several other specialized and temporary structures which are not of great relevance and, consequently, we can confine ourselves to mentioning them briefly. These are houses of an intermediate form between the tent and the igloo. They are only used regularly in the central regions. In Baffin Land, in spring, when the vault of the snow-house begins to melt and before it is possible to live again in a tent, the Eskimo construct igloos with walls made of snow but with a dome formed of skins; among others, see Parry (1824, p. 358) for a good description. Conversely, at the beginning of winter, the tent is sometimes covered with turf, shrubs and moss; skins are then placed over this initial covering and a vault of snow is erected at the entrance. Sometimes this structure remains; see Boas (1888, pp. 551, 553). Virtually everywhere the Eskimo make use of these intermediate structures, especially when in the course of a trek, even in summer, a period of bad weather forces them to construct a shelter. Kane (1856, p. 46) describes these intermediate structures at Disco in 1851. We should also mention that small houses and tents are generally used to isolate a tabooed woman. On Point Barrow, see especially Murdoch (1892, p. 86); see also Woolfe in Porter (1893, p. 141). This is one example of the effect of social physiology on morphology and there are others as well. We are leaving out the summer houses in Alaska, since this question is a little too technical to be discussed here.
77 The figures cited above on Eskimo settlement relate to winter settlements. The concentration of all 'social unity' on one point eventually results in a maximum concentration. See the discussion in Rink (1877, vol. 2, p. 253) and very good descriptions in Cranz (1765, XII, 1, 4 and 5), Boas (1888, pp. 482 ff., 561) and Schanz, Woolfe and Porter in Porter (1893, pp. 102 ff., 148, 164).
78 Winter movements are not common except in Baffin Land; see Boas (1901, p. 421). The map of these movements provided by Boas (Map II) ought not, however, to mislead us about the extent of these movements.
79 The only tribe that constitutes a relative exception to this rule is the one at Smith Strait; see Kroeber (1899, pp. 41 ff.) and Peary (1898, vol. 1, pp. 502 ff.). But we have explained that there are special conditions involved for this tribe.
80 See Table 1 in chapter 1, and Holm (1887, pp. 89 ff.).
81 Tales in particular preserve the theme about individuals who live in isolated houses, but this is precisely because of the romantic character of this kind of life; see Rink (1875, pp. 278, 568 [?]) and Boas (1901, p. 202). Hayes (1860, pp. 242-4) explains the existence

of isolated individuals on Northumberland Island, Smith Strait: the wife of one individual is a sorceress.

82 Petroff (1884, pp. 125-6 ff.).
83 See Petroff (1884, appendix II) and the texts cited in chapter 1 n. 51 above.
84 See nn. 49 and 50 to this chapter and Sverdrup (1903, vol. 1, p. 150; vol. 2, p. 179; maps: vol. 1, p. 320; vol. 2, p. 128). In these regions there are also ruins of houses which were grouped together; see Sverdrup (1903, vol. 1, p. 211; vol. 2, p. 371).
85 The majority of texts cited in nn. 41-56 of this chapter are drawn from descriptions of winter settlements to which we refer for the last time. Steensby (1905, pp. 51-141) also gives numerous references which we need not list.
86 The plans of Lichtenfels and Neu Herrnhut provided in Cranz (1765, II) come from European missionaries.
87 Rasbinsky in Nelson (1899, p. 247), Jacobsen (1884, p. 324) and Porter (1893, p. 107). One, a winter village facing a summer village, was certainly constructed under Russian influence.
88 See n. 5 of this chapter. The text by Coats which discusses the only 'case' is evidently exaggerated.
89 See Richardson in Franklin (1828, pp. 215-16) and Richardson (1851, vol. 1, pp. 254-5). In the north of Melville Peninsula, the ruins are all connected; see Bellot (1854, p. 207). In his discussion of Netchillirmiut igloos, Richardson (1851, vol. 1, p. 350) says: 'Social intercourse is promoted by building houses contiguously, and cutting doors of communication between them, or by erecting covered passages'. It is quite remarkable that at Cook Inlet, at the point where Indian and Eskimo societies meet, there exists a village in which all the winter houses are connected with the *kashim*; see Jacobsen (1884, p. 362).
90 There is a great deal of general information on a large number of summer camps in Steensby (1905, pp. 50-130, 142 ff.).
91 For meteorological details, see Kornerup (1880, pp. 28 ff.), Holm (1887-8, pp. 227 ff.) and Warming (1888, pp. 139 ff.).
92 See the descriptions in Nansen (1903, pp. 72 ff.), H. P. Egede (1729, p. 25; 1741, p. 90), Cranz (1765, III, 1, 5) and Rink (1875, p. 7; 1866-71; suppl., p. xiii). The stories clearly indicate the passage from winter to summer; see Rink (1875, pp. 189, 132).
93 Cranz (1770, p. 247).
94 In the southern districts, large camps are formed to fish for capelin, but they are quite temporary and transient.
95 See Rink (1875, vol. 2, pp. 250 ff.).
96 It is possible to extract the history of the dispersions and periodic movements from accounts of different missions during the first years of their establishment: for Labrador, see *Periodical Accounts*, and for Greenland, Cranz (1765, V; 1770, pp. 4 ff.) and P. H. Egede (1741; 1788, p. 245). There is not enough space here to publish this research which we have done.
97 For maps from Chesterfield Inlet to Repulse Bay, see Parry (1824,

p. 195, plate facing p. 198).

98 See Parry (1824, pp. 269, 279) and Lyon (1824, p. 343).

99 For the migration of the tribes of Baffin Land and the area of their dispersion during the summer, see Boas (1888, pp. 421 ff.), where he summarizes the majority of texts.

100 There is a great deal of information in almost all the voyagers' accounts. Among others, see Franklin (1828, pp. 120–1) and especially those who were sent in search of Franklin. They made their explorations during the summer and everywhere they found abandoned winter villages, scattered tents and dispersed camps. We do not have the space to indicate all the references; these are already provided by Steensby (1905). We may simply add to his and to those of Boas the following: Hanbury (1904, pp. 42, 124, 126, 127, 142, 144, 145, 176, 214, 216) and Tyrrell (1898, pp. 105, 110), which cover the least known regions between Chesterfield Inlet and the Mackenzie.

101 On these journeys, some of which extended over two years, see Murdoch (1892, pp. 43, 45) and the texts cited; also Simpson (1875, p. 243) and Woolfe in Porter (1893, p. 137).

102 Petitot (1887, p. 28). The majority, however, are meeting-points for trading with Europeans or Indians; elsewhere we find the same tribes completely dispersed; see Petitot (1887, pp. 166, 167, 179). Hooper (1853, p. 260) reports a large camp of two hundred tents in July 1850 at Herschel Island. See also MacClure (1853, p. 92).

103 Hooper (1853, p. 348 and illustration facing p. 350) and Richardson (1851, vol. 1, p. 248).

104 Equally temporary phenomena explain the larger camps observed by Beechey (1831, vol. 1, pp. 247, 256), which are quite close to other small camps.

105 On these villages, rather than Nelson (1899, pp. 285 ff.), see Schanz and Weber in Porter (1893, pp. 180 ff.).

106 The village observed by Nelson (1899, p. 261) at Hotham Inlet is a temporary trading village. For other similar instances, see Woolfe in Porter (1893, p. 137) and Murdoch (1892, p. 80).

107 For these villages, see Nelson (1899, pp. 242 ff.) who limits the existence of permanent summer villages to the Kuskokwim region.

108 See Porter (1893, p. 123) and Elliott (1886, pp. 402, 404). The Togiagmiut, according to Jacobsen (1884, p. 347) and Elliott (1886, p. 401), still lived in summer tents although they were affected by the same conditions as the Kuskokwgmiut, the Kvikkpagmiut, Ikogmiut, etc. We therefore surmise that the use of the house and the summer village constructed of wood originated with the Russians in these regions.

109 Ratzel (1895, pp. 163 ff.; 1897, pp. 263–7; 1899, vol. 1, pp. 217 ff.); see also Durkheim (1901, p. 565).

110 See Boas (1888, p. 421) and Figure 6 above; see also the map in Parry (1824, plate facing p. 198). The major expeditions by Hall and Schwatka to the Boothia Peninsula and King William Land and by Hanbury over the entire arctic coast were made in company

with Eskimo families.

111 The most remarkable voyage is that of some people from Baffin Land to Smith Strait and of their attempt to return; see Rasmussen (1905, pp. 21 ff.) and Boas (1888, pp. 443, 459). The Eskimo frequently crossed from western to southern Greenland; see Holm (1888, p. 56).

112 Parry (1824, pp. xiii, 185, 195, 198, 251, 253, 276, 513, 514), Lyon (1824, pp. 160, 161, 177, 250), Franklin (1828, p. 132, dealing with Herschel Island), Petitot (1887, p. 73, which is absurd), Beechey (1831, vol. 2, pp. 291, 331), Miertsching (1864, p. 83), Hall (1864, vol. 2, pp. 331, 342), Boas (1888, pp. 643-8), Holm (1888, tables, woodcuts on plate XXXI) and Simpson, *Discoveries on the Shores of the Arctic Sea*, p. 149. [Reference uncertain, possibly either T. Simpson (1843) or Dease and Simpson (1838 and 1839). JJF.]

Chapter 3   The causes of Eskimo seasonal variations

1 In any case, we must do away with the classic notion of the 'arctic house' which is still found in Berghaus (1850-2, p. 67).

2 See the isotherms, even for winter, in Bartholomew (1899, map XVII), although the cold pole of Werchoïansk (Siberia) should be omitted. See also *Geogr. Jour.* 1904. [Specific reference uncertain, probably Mackinder. JJF.]

3 Hearne, one of the first explorers, drew this opposition (1795, pp. 160, 162), as did Coats (1852, p. 33); see also Petitot (1887, p. 26).

4 Jacobsen (1884) specifically notes the greater endurance of the Indians of Alaska.

5 See Porter (1893, p. 103) and Elliott (1886, p. 405).

6 Steensby (1905, p. 105, thesis 2; pp. 199 ff.).

7 Except among the Eskimo of Point Barrow (Murdoch, 1892, p. 344), snowshoes have not been in use for very long and may even have been imported. In any case, those mentioned by Kumlien (1879, p. 42) and Boas (1901, p. 41) are certainly rare and of recent origin, probably imported by whalers. Their use has been spread by Europeans in Greenland and by the Eskimo from Baffin Land to Smith Strait. According to Maclean (1849, vol. 1, p. 139), the Eskimo were confined to the coast just because of their lack of snowshoes. Steensby (1905, p. 10) speaks somewhat incorrectly of 'snesko', probably referring to the waterproof boot. The only exception is that of the Nooatok of Alaska, but they are intermixed with Indians and, since they can follow game, live in the interior; furthermore they have a morphology that is quite similar to that of the Cree or the Tinneh. See Wells and Kelly (1890, pp. 14-15, 26-7), Porter (1893, p. 125) and Nelson (1899, p. 18). But we know practically nothing else about this tribe.

8 In 1822 there was practically no summer at Iglulik; the people remarked on this to Parry and told him that they did not disperse to hunt reindeer; see Parry (1824, p. 357).

9 The preceding description is, in large part, similar to that given by Boas (1888, pp. 419–20); see also Richardson (1861, pp. 300 ff.). The Eskimo of Point Barrow who live by hunting reindeer during the winter constitute the exception which actually confirms the rule, because they can do this thanks to their snowshoes; see Simpson (1875, pp. 261–3) and Murdoch (1892, pp. 45 ff.).

10 We are not considering for the time being the question of the length of arctic days and nights. Whereas the darkness causes a general slowing down in animal and vegetable life, the enormous impact of the summer sun effects an incomparable growth. On this point see G. Andersson (1902) and Rikli (1903).

11 For lack of space, we cannot discuss here the progressions and variations through which this dispersion and spreading out occurs. But it would be a pity not to quote Parry's description (1824, p. 534) of the perfect accord and the automatic nature of these movements: 'In all their movements they seem to be actuated by one simultaneous feeling that is truly admirable.'

Chapter 4   The effects of Eskimo seasonal variations

1 We will not make every effort here, as we did with morphology, to provide a table of every Eskimo law and religious practice, nor to give a list of equivalents of every custom in each Eskimo society whether well known or not, nor to indicate, when we lack such equivalents, the cause of the absence of this or that fact. The task would be difficult if not impossible, and, given the nature of our subject, misleading as well. It is enough for us to recall the remarkable unity of the whole of Eskimo culture (see Introduction, n. 2), and it will be enough for us to show the extent of some of the main phenomena and to indicate, as we proceed, their different effects in the diverse societies, so that we can draw our conclusions.

Neither have we troubled to provide a description of the two technologies of summer and winter, whose contrast is just as great as the two systems of law or religion. Steensby (1905, pp. 142 ff.) has dealt with this question very well.

2 European travellers who either passed through Eskimo territory or who stayed in one place and were unable to follow Eskimo migrations have provided very little information on summer religious activities. They tell us nothing and we can draw our own conclusion. The collective summer festivities in Alaska (see Woolfe in Porter (1893, pp. 141–2) and Nelson (1899, p. 295)) and in Greenland (see Cranz (1765, IV, 1, 5) and the tales, which are partially fantasy, in Rink (1875, pp. 125, 137 ff.)) are quite simply exceptions that are associated with markets. The festivities held in June at Point Barrow (see Murdoch (1892, p. 375) and Woolfe in Porter (1893, p. 142)) are the result of whale-hunting that extends

the duration of the winter group. Moreover, these festivities appear to be distinct from the 'formal' festivals of winter; see Murdoch (1892, p. 365).

3 These are sometimes different in summer and winter. On provisional naming among the Unalit, see Nelson (1899, p. 289). For the custom at Angmagssalik, see n. 24 in this chapter.

4 These are naturally different depending on the number and nature of the populations and objects involved. On Ungava, see Turner (1894, p. 193); on Greenland, see H. P. Egede (1741, pp. 82-3).

5 The description of the majority of performances by *angekok* refer to houses and, hence, to the winter. See, however, Parry (1824, p. 369). Holm (1888, p. 123) says of Angmagssalik: 'De rigtige Angekokkunster foregaa kun om Vinteren'. ['The true *angekok* artist performs only in winter.']

6 For these performances in Greenland, see Egede (1729, p. 45; 1741, p. 115) and Cranz (1765, III, 5, 39 and 41), who says that the magician cannot make his tour among the Torngarsuk before the autumn and that this tour is shortest in winter. In Rink (1875, pp. 37, 60), the great art appears to be restricted to the winter. For Labrador, see Turner (1894, pp. 194 ff.); for the central regions, see Boas (1888, pp. 592 ff.; 1901, pp. 121, 128 ff., 240: tale 53) and Hall (1864, vol. 2, p. 319); for the Mackenzie, see Petitot (1876, p. xxiv); for Point Barrow, Murdoch (1892, pp. 430 ff.); for the western Eskimo, Simpson (1875, p. 271), and for Alaska, Nelson (1899, pp. 435 ff.).

7 Nelson (1899, pp. 284, 288) and Woolfe in Porter (1893, p. 149).

8 Parry (1824, p. 509) and Hall (1864, vol. 2, pp. 182, 197).

9 For the central Eskimo, see Boas (1888, p. 611: 'It is a busy season'. [604: 'It is then a busy season for the wizards.' JJF.]; 1901, pp. 121 ff.). For a striking anecdote, see Rasmussen (1905, p. 29).

10 H. P. Egede (1741, pp. 85 ff.) and Cranz (1765, III, 5, 3 ff.); see also the reports on Neu Herrnhut.

11 On confession, see Boas (1901, pp. 128 ff.) and Lewis (1904, p. 63); Lyon (1824, pp. 357 ff.) notes the same facts.

12 For this reason it is probably necessary to have an *angekok* in the winter settlement. For Smith Sound, see Rasmussen (1905, p. 161) and for western Greenland, Cranz (1767, vol. 2, p. 304, note).

13 See Petroff (1884, p. 132), Wells and Kelly (1890, p. 24) and Schanz in Porter (1893, p. 94).

14 For the Nugumiut, the *kashim* is dedicated to a spirit, and consequently all that occurs there has a religious character; see Boas (1888, p. 601; 1901, pp. 148, 332: tale). In Greenland, the word that signifies a festival and an assembly contains the radical '*qagse*'. See references cited in chapter 2 n. 66 above.

15 Nelson (1899, pp. 285 ff., 388 ff.), Murdoch (1892, p. 374) and Boas (1888, p. 602).

16 Nelson (1899, pp. 368 ff.), Elliott (1886, pp. 393 ff.), Zagoskin in Petroff (1884), Woolfe in Porter (1893, p. 143) and Wells and

Kelly (1890, p. 24); also Murdoch (1892, p. 434) and the comparisons made in the notes.

17 Nelson (1899, pp. 358 ff.).

18 Woolfe in Porter (1893, pp. 140-1); for the festival at Ignitkok, see Jacobsen (1884, p. 260). These two travellers make the same error and do not appreciate the idea of namesakes. See Wassilieff in Wrangell (1839, p. 130) and Elliott (1886, pp. 390, 393); also Zagoskin's report in Petroff (1884, p. 130) and Wells and Kelly (1890). We have no information about the presence or absence of this ritual at Point Barrow. For the central regions as far as Chesterfield Inlet, we have little information; see, however, Petitot (1887, pp. 156, 167), which is dubious. For the central Eskimo, see Boas (1888, pp. 608, 610, 628 n. 6; 1901, pp. 146, 148, and tales on pp. 186, 330), Hall (1864, vol. 2, p. 120), Kumlien (1879, p. 48), Lewis (1904, pp. 41 ff. (the tribe at Fort Churchill) and p. 242 (Blacklead Island)). As for Greenland, we know only the outlines of the ritual; see P. H. Egede (1750, p. 5: 'Attekkessiorok, dat cui quid nominis gratia'). For Labrador, see Erdmann (1864, p. 20, col. 2; p. 42). See also Rink (1875, pp. 281 ff., tale no. 47), which deals with a ritual offering to a child who has the same name as the deceased, and Cranz (1770, pp. 110, 334).

19 On the Nugumiut, see Hall (1864, vol. 2, p. 320), also Boas (1888, p. 606). In our opinion, the rite called the extinguishing of the lamps, which occurs throughout Greenland, is, according to observers, nothing more than a rite of sexual licence often associated with a séance of the winged *angekok* which probably once accompanied the sun festival summarily noted by Cranz (1765, III, 3, 23 and 24); see n. 89 in this chapter. On the exchange of women that follows the extinguishing of the lamps among the Qumarmiut, see S. Rink (1900, p. 44: 'som Skik var over hele Kysten baade hvergang det var Nymaane og efter visse Fester': 'as was customarily done along the entire coast at each new moon or after certain festivals').

20 See pp. 62 ff.

21 Boas (1888, p. 604, Appendix, note 6; 1901, p. 141).

22 Boas (1888, p. 611; 1901, p. 140). Hall (1864, vol. 2, p. 313) alludes to this rite which consists in pressing a bird's skin onto the head of the child, after its birth.

23 A text in Boas (1901, p. 140) allows this conjecture.

24 Holm (1888, p. 91); see also the obscure text in H. P. Egede (1741, p. 81).

25 We allude to the myth of Sedna, examples of which, we believe, can be found throughout Eskimo culture. Sedna appears to be the primary mythological figure assigned to explain and sanction the taboos concerning sea animals and, consequently among others, the seasonal taboos. For this myth, see Lyon (1824, p. 362), Boas (1888, pp. 583 ff.; 1901, pp. 120, 145 ff., 163) and Hall (1864, vol. 2, p. 321). On the distribution and origin of this myth, see Boas (1904), and for my review of Boas, see Mauss (1905).

26 Beliefs such as those that underlie the tale from Greenland concerning Igludtsialek are precisely the product of these taboos and of a Sedna myth which is entirely autochthonous. The female *angekok* requests her 'summer dress' to go up into the mountains to break up and destroy the ice; see Rink (1875, pp. 150 ff.).

27 Hall (1864, vol. 2, p. 321) and Boas (1901, p. 122), also Tyrrell (1898, pp. 169 ff.) and Lewis (1904, pp. 43, 122). In Hanbury (1904, pp. 46 ff., 69, 97, 100), there are some very interesting details about the injunction against working reindeer-skin on the ice or sealskin on land, etc.

28 Boas (1901, p. 122) and Hall (1864, vol. 1, pp. 201-2). Something that happened by chance to the founders of the Labrador Mission demonstrates that the same belief was current there; see *The Moravians in Labrador* (1833, pp. 21-2, 100).

29 Boas (1901, p. 123).

30 Boas (1901, p. 123); see also the myth mentioned in Boas (1888, pp. 587-8). It appears, moreover, that the myth has taken various forms, even among the Aivilik; see Hanbury (1904).

31 Boas (1901, p. 124).

32 Boas (1901, p. 124).

33 Boas (1901, p. 122).

34 See Durkheim and Mauss (1903). In exactly the same way the Zuñi seem to have classified things into those of summer and those of winter in accordance with their two phratries. Among the Eskimo, the division into things of the sea and things of the land appears to us to coincide with that between summer and winter.

35 See Durkheim (1902).

36 This opposition has already been noted by Parry (1824, p. 534), Lyon (1824, p. 250), Boas (1888, pp. 562 ff.), Lewis (1904, p. 52), Richardson (1861, pp. 318 ff.), Glasunov in Wrangell (1839, pp. 130 ff.) and (for Alaska) by Schanz in Porter (1893, p. 106); and see also the generalizations by Petroff (1884, pp. 125 ff.). Moreover, although the excellent books by Rink (1875, pp. 23 ff.; 1887, p. 26), Nelson (1899) and Murdoch (1892) do not expressly mention this opposition, they provide a considerable number of facts that support our theory. There is also a gap in the work of Steensby, who recognized the opposition of the two technologies but did not see that of the two legal structures of Eskimo society.

37 For western Greenland, Cumberland Sound and Churchill River, see Morgan (1871, pp. 275 ff.). Another list from Cumberland Sound was published by Dall (1877, pp. 95 ff.).

38 See n. 50 in this chapter.

39 On the composition of the summer family, see Rink (1875, pp. 20 ff.) and Turner (1894, p. 183).

40 The role of provider was recognized by the first Danish authors; see Cranz (1765, III, 3 and 4 and the numerous facts mentioned in the reports for 1738, 1743, etc.).

41 See Rink (1875, p. 28 and the tales on p. 169).

42 Unless someone has marriageable daughters. If the children are

very young, they seem to be regularly put to death. For contrary evidence, see Murdoch (1892, p. 318), but, as is well known, the population at Point Barrow is extremely reduced.

43 Rink (1875, p. 24) and Holm (1888, p. 97).

44 Rink (1875, p. 24), Turner (1894, p. 190 which is particularly clear), Hall (1864, vol. 1, p. 370), Boas (1888, pp. 545 ff.) and Nelson (1899, pp. 285 ff.).

45 Rink (1875, p. 25), Holm (1888, p. 88) and Boas (1888, p. 566).

46 See chapter 1, n. 10. Lyon (1824, p. 353) also mentions the fact that a young widow would be available to all the members of the settlement for some time before she was put to death.

47 This latter fact could serve to explain another one that is curious and, at first sight, disconcerting: the absolute independence of the child and the respect that parents have for it; see the texts cited above in chapter 1, n. 40 and nn. 17 and 18 in this chapter. They never strike a child and even obey a child's orders. The child is not just the hope of the family, in the sense that we would give to that word today, but the reincarnation of an ancestor. Within the restricted, isolated and autonomous summer family, the child is like the pole that attracts beliefs and interests.

48 The first comparison between the moral order of the Eskimo long-house and of the Indian house was made by Rink (1887, p. 23); see also Tyrrell (1898, p. 68).

49 See Morgan (1871, pp. 275 ff.).

50 See Rink (1887, pp. 93 ff.) with equivalent terms, and P. H. Egede (1750, p. 32: *iglu*), Kleinschmidt (1871, p. 75: *igdlo*), Erdmann (1864, pp. 52, 63) and Petitot (1876, p. xliii). See also Egede (1729, p. 45).

51 Rink (1877 [?], vol. 2, pp. 9, 26) and Petitot (1876, p. xxix).

52 Murdoch (1892, p. 75).

53 Jacobsen (1884, pp. 240-1). Most of the '*meillagers*' are people adopted by the quasi-chief, Isaac. See the description of the winter family in Holm (1888, p. 66: Table XXIII and, for names and genealogies, p. 95).

54 Rink (1875, p. 25). See also H. P. Egede (1741, p. 79); Cranz (1765, III, 2, 13), Holm (1888, pp. 85, 94), Turner (1894, pp. 188-9) and Boas (1888, p. 579). For contrary evidence, see Lyon (1824, pp. 352-4) and Wells and Kelly (1890, p. 22): these are certainly inaccurate and perhaps allude to sexual licence.

55 From Egede to Holm (1888, p. 194), all Danish writers have used the term, '*sammenbragde*'. Egede (1729, p. 79) adds something that does not occur subsequently, 'in dit saadan Huse'. In Rink (1875, p. 291), there is a tale of a boy who is supposed to have married his adopted sister in Greenland; but the adoption was recent and the children had not been brought up together.

56 Moreover, in Point Barrow, cousins are often regarded as brother and sister; see Murdoch (1892, p. 421).

57 Nelson (1899, p. 291).

58 One can even extract from the genealogy given in Holm (1888, p.

95) the fact that the cousins Angitinguak (m.), Angmalilik (m.), Kutuluk (f.) and Nakitilik (f.) all married people from their settlement, and their children also married within the settlement where they had settled.

59 Nelson (1899, p. 291).

60 On the totemic clan of the Unalit and its exogamy, see Nelson (1899, pp. 322 ff.).

61 In Rink (1875, pp. 25-6), the existence of genuine heads of houses is really reported only for northern Alaska. See also Simpson (1875, p. 272), Murdoch (1892, p. 429), Petroff (1884, p. 125) and Woolfe in Porter (1893, p. 135).

62 On this point, see Rink (1875, pp. 26, 54; 1887, p. 22), also Cranz (1770, p. 329).

63 *Nunaqatigit* in the Greenland language. See Rink (1891, p. 93, section 29) and the various dictionaries.

64 Reinforced by the continual communal feast which constitutes life in the *kashim* or in the winter igloos.

65 See p. 47 above.

66 Egede (1729, p. 37; 1741, p. 91), Cranz (1765, III, 3, 20), Dalager (1758), Coats (1852, p. 76: 'gentle and sociable'; see chapter 2 n. 1 in this book), Parry (1824, pp. 500, 533), who deals with both the moral regime of the winter settlement and that of the winter long-house, and Wassilieff and Glasunov in Wrangell (1839, p. 129). We refer only to the older authors because later remarks have since become completely stylized; see Nansen (1903, pp. 293 ff., 138 ff.).

67 See especially Cranz (1765, III, 4, 28). Nelson (1899, pp. 301 ff.) gives a kind of historical picture made up of diverse facts from Alaska in 1881-2.

68 Rink (1875, p. 34).

69 See examples in Murdoch (1892, p. 420), Simpson (1875, p. 252), Parry (1824, p. 529: the Iglulik), Woolfe in Porter (1893, p. 135) and Wells and Kelly (1890, p. 19). Fidelity in marriage appears to these latter authors to be contrary to the custom of wife exchange, but no such contradiction exists.

70 Rink (1875, pp. 34 ff.; 1887, p. 24), Nelson (1899, p. 293), Schanz in Porter (1893, p. 103), Boas (1888, p. 582; 1901, p. 116) and Lewis (1904, p. 32).

71 Rink (1875, pp. 35-6). It is expressly stated that threatening the life of a 'housemate' is not liable to blood vengeance. But, to the contrary, see the numerous tales in Rink (1875: no. 30 on pp. 224 ff.; 38 on pp. 255 ff., etc.). See also Hanbury (1904, p. 46). Tyrrell (1898, p. 170) mentions a rule (for Labrador?, Chesterfield Inlet?) which requires a murderer simply to adopt the family of his victim; we suspect this comes from some confusion with Indian practice. However, see Boas (1901, p. 118) for data that could have given rise to the error.

72 See examples in the tales in Rink (1875: no. 22: Angutisugssuk, etc.) and Boas (1901, pp. 72 ff.).

73 See H. P. Egede (1729, p. 43; 1741, p. 86), Cranz (1765, III, 3,

23), Rink (1875, pp. 33, 67), Holm (1888, pp. 157 ff.; tales nos 47 ff. which deal with Angmagssalik) and Rasmussen (1905: Cape York and Smith Sound).

74 See Steinmetz (1892, p. 67). According to Tylor (1883–4, p. 268), the songs might be of Scandinavian origin. This is possible. But it is difficult to assert a European origin for the public reproach practised in Alaska (Nelson, 1899, p. 293) which results in the execution of the sentence. And a parallel practice could easily give rise to the Greenland custom. On the other hand, there are no other exact Eskimo equivalents; see examples from Fort Churchill in Franklin (1828, pp. 182, 197); see also Tyrrell (1898, p. 132) and Gilder (1881, p. 245).

75 See Cranz (1765, III, 4, 33).

76 Rink (1875, pp. 34–5), Holm (1888, p. 58); see also Nelson (1899, p. 430).

77 Rink (1875, pp. 34–5).

78 Boas (1901, pp. 121 ff.). See, however, an anecdote in Rasmussen (1905, p. 31) about the daughter of an *angekok* from Baffin Land abandoned by her father because she did not confess to having violated a taboo.

79 Boas (1901, pp. 121 ff.).

80 Rink (1875, p. 34) and Nelson (1899, pp. 291 ff.). For a remarkable rite (a declaration of war?), see Wells and Kelly (1890, p. 24) and Wassilieff in Wrangell (1839, p. 132).

81 Rink (1875, p. 35 and tales on pp. 174–5, 235, 206–7, and p. 211 in contrast to pp. 357–8). On tribes to the north versus those to the south, see Schultz-Lorentzen (1904, p. 320).

82 Boas (1888, p. 465; 1901, p. 116, tales nos 72 ff.), Kumlien (1879, p. 12) and Klutschak (1881, p. 228).

83 Holm (1888, p. 87) and S. Rink (1900, p. 45).

84 Rink (1875, p. 157, tales nos 39 and 40).

85 Boas (1888, pp. 465, 609; 1901, p. 116); see also Klutschak (1881, pp. 67 ff.), Schwatka (1884).

86 Nelson (1899, pp. 294 ff.).

87 Boas (1888, p. 609; 1901, p. 609). See also the tales about the bloody end of a ball game in Rink (1875, pp. 211, 226).

88 On the widespread exchange of women among the Eskimo, see Richardson (1861, p. 319) and Murdoch (1892, p. 413).

89 H. P. Egede (1741, p. 78) and P. Egede (1750, p. 100) on the word *malliserpok*. If Cranz does not mention this custom in his description, it is because of his tendency to be an apologist; but he mentions an 'extinguishing of the lamps' ritual in connection with whale-hunting (1765, III, 5, 43). In the report of the Mission we find other traces of it, for example in 1743; see Cranz (1767, vol. 2, p. 70). It is indeed remarkable that Rink neither mentions this custom nor has left a tale which properly relates to it, except perhaps for the universal Eskimo tale about the incest of the sun and moon (1875, p. 236). In the versions of the tale which we consider the most primitive, this incest always occurs in a *kashim*

and naturally at the time of the extinguishing of the lamps. See the bibliography on this tale in Boas (1901, p. 359); see also Thalbitzer (1904, p. 275). This is very important because it demonstrates that the scene indeed occurs as we say; see Rasmussen (1905, p. 194).

90 See n. 19 in this chapter. See also Petitot (1887, p. 166) and Lewis (1904, pp. 55, 242). This exchange occurs after every *angekok* ceremony at Kinipetu. See Boas (1901, pp. 139, 158), Klutschak (1881a, p. 210) and Turner (1894, pp. 178, 200). The only probable exception is the tribe at Point Barrow where Murdoch searched vainly (perhaps insufficiently) for this practice (1892, p. 375). The custom of temporary exchange is practised, in any case, and Murdoch compares this to communal sex (1892, p. 415).

91 The prohibition on sexual relations between consanguines appears to be respected. See Holm (1888, p. 98) and the tale about the sun and moon already cited in n. 89 above.

92 Wrangell (1839) describes the way in which old women in the lower Yukon region offer themselves by virtue of distant kinship relations. But the practice is perhaps the same as that cited below.

93 Hall (1864, vol. 2, p. 323), Lewis (1904, p. 41) and Boas (1901, pp. 139, 158).

94 For the Ikogmiut, see Nelson (1899, pp. 379, 494).

95 Moreover, from this latter point of view, a temporary exchange amounts to the same thing; see Murdoch (1892, p. 419) and Porter (1893, p. 39).

96 See Weber in Porter (1893, p. 103), Wells and Kelly (1890, p. 19), Murdoch (1892, p. 413), Parry (1824, p. 300) (who reports an anecdote about the *angekok* Toolemak) and Lyon (1824, p. 354), who speaks of the exchanging of sisters that is quite possible.

97 See Lyon (1824, p. 354).

98 Parry (1824, p. 530), Murdoch (1892, pp. 413, 419), Boas (1888, p. 579), Kumlien (1879, p. 42) and Lewis (1904, p. 55).

99 The *angekok* even appears to have a special right; see the anecdote in Parry (1824, p. 300); also Turner (1894, p. 200).

100 Peary (1898, vol. 1, p. 497) and Kroeber (1899, p. 56).

101 Peary (1898, vol. 1, p. 497). Rasmussen does not mention this detail in his excellent description of the exchange of women (1905, p. 64).

102 Kane (1856, vol. 2, p. 211).

103 Nelson (1899, p. 493) and Porter (1893, p. 103). Naturally this does not preclude those exchanges within the settlement which result in the same rights. See also Wells and Kelly (1890, p. 29).

104 Nelson (1899, p. 493).

105 The same terms are used as those for natural kin in Greenland. The American census-takers are convinced that the mingling of rights and of blood is so complete that the establishment of genealogies is almost impossible.

106 Nansen (1903, pp. 146, 204 no. 1); see also the obscure information from Klutschak (1881a, p. 234).

107 See n. 58 in this chapter.

108 Nelson does not in fact mention this in regard to the Unalit. And it is very remarkable that in the masked festivities of the neighbouring tribes (Ahpokagamiut, Ikogmiut), women are exchanged without regard to kinship; see Porter (1893, p. 103) and Nelson (1899, pp. 379, 494).

109 See Rink (1875, p. 28).

110 See Cranz (1765, III, 3, 22) and Boas (1888, p. 577).

111 For all that follows, particularly in regard to Greenland, see Dalager (1758), H. P. Egede (1741, p. 81, which is less precise), Cranz (1765, III, 3, 25, which follows Dalager) and Rink (1875, pp. 10 ff., 22 ff.). It seems that Danish writers all refer to a codification of information compiled just once by Dalager, H. P. Egede and the Moravian Brethren, at the beginning of the European settlements. See Cranz (1765, X, sections 4, 5, 6 and the reports from Neu Herrnhut for 1746, 1750; 1767, vol. 2, pp. 88, 142). Nordenskiöld (1885, pp. 500 ff.) and Nansen (1903, p. 106) only repeat information from other Danish writers.

112 Among the central and western Eskimo, she always takes it with her in the event of divorce.

113 Rink (1875, p. 30), Holm (1888, p. 118) and Nelson (1899, p. 137).

114 Cranz (1765, III, 3, 25).

115 We are not aware of a single exception to this rule among all the writers who have discussed the Eskimo; we therefore refrain from providing references.

116 On property marks and their distribution, see Boas (1899, pp. 602 ff.) and Hoffman (1897, pp. 720 ff.) [?]. The distribution of these property marks certainly goes beyond the Mackenzie region; see Petitot (1887, p. 187). Boas states that they are not known in Baffin Land nor to the north-west of Hudson Bay; see, however, (1901, p. 94). But, without assuming the necessity of physical marks, it is certain that hunting rights as precise as those of the Eskimo could not be employed unless each hunter had some means of proving which weapon was his. See Dalager in Cranz (1765, III, 3, 25) as well as p. 75 above.

117 On the power of the totem, see Nelson (1899, pp. 323 ff.).

118 Nelson (1899, p. 438); see also Chappell (1817, p. 65).

119 Lyon (1824, p. 21); Chappell (1817, p. 55).

120 Anecdote in Nansen (1903, p. 91). European snowshoes are not subject to ordinary rules.

121 It is buried with her; see Boas (1888, p. 580).

122 See Rink (1875, p. 30), Turner (1894, p. 105) and Boas (1888, p. 541).

123 Rink (1875, pp. 23, 28).

124 Examples in Hall (1864, vol. 1, p. 250).

125 See chapter 1 n. 75.

126 See the tales in Boas (1901, pp. 172, 202, 211, 239, etc.).

127 See Cranz (1765, III, 3, 25), Rink (1875, pp. 10, 23), Holm (1888, pp. 83 ff.), Boas (1888, pp. 581 ff.), Murdoch (1892, p. 85), Petitot (1876, p. xxxi), Richardson (1861, p. 319), Woolfe in Porter (1893, p. 137) and Petroff (1884, p. 125).

128 Holm (1888, p. 87), S. Rink (1900, p. 51), Cranz (1765, III, 3, 25; X, 7), Dalager (1758), P. H. Egede (1788), Rink (1875, p. 27, who formally states that this is a rule for the winter settlement) and Nansen (1903, pp. 91 ff., who repeats Dalager, and introduces some errors). At Smith Strait, the communalism seems both absolute and limited exclusively to *bopladfaeller*; see the anecdote in Rasmussen (1905, p. 81), also Nordenskiöld (1885, p. 503), Boas (1888, p. 577), Hall (1864, vol. 2, p. 290), Klutschak (1881a, p. 66), Kumlien (1879, p. 18), Petitot (1876, p. xxxii) and Porter (1893, pp. 103, 137, 141, etc.). Nelson and Murdoch have nothing to say on this subject.

129 S. Rink (1900, p. 51) and Rink (1875, pp. 26 ff.).

130 Rink (1875, p. 26), Dalager (1758), Cranz (1765, III, 3, 5), H. P. Egede (1741, p. 91), Boas (1888, p. 587: limited to strangers).

131 Nelson (1899, p. 285) says the same, that the *kashim* may be built by several villages of the same tribe and that this reinforces their feelings of friendship. Simpson (1875, p. 259) says that all *kashim* are the property of particular individuals. See also Parry (1824, p. 360). Murdoch (1892, p. 79) denies this.

132 Boas (1888, p. 577), Hall (1879, p. 226) and Klutschak (1881a, p. 234).

133 Rasmussen's history of the Eskimo of Baffin Land states that these Eskimo introduced to the tribe at Smith Strait a communal rite of passing the bone (1905, p. 32); see also Hall (1864, vol. 1, p. 170; vol. 2, p. 120; 1879, p. 226) and Lyon (1824, pp. 125, 127).

134 Rink (1875, p. 28); or, rather, everyone in the district comes of their own accord, according to Dalager (1758). On Point Barrow, see Murdoch (1892, p. 438).

135 Rink (1875, p. 29). We are not saying that this whale-hunting takes place in winter, nor that the stranding of dead whales occurs in this season; we simply think that this right ought to be compared with the right of the assembled community in regard to smaller whales which applies especially in winter.

136 Rink (1875, p. 29), who repeats Cranz and Dalager.

137 Rink (1875, p. 29) and Nelson (1899, p. 294).

138 Rink (1875, p. 30). For Labrador, see Stearns (1884, p. 256); for central Eskimo, see Parry (1824, p. 530); Lyon (1824, pp. 302, 348-9). Lyon's account has a minor error of observation but his remark about the feeling of envy in the community is quite significant.

139 See Rink (1875, pp. 27, 132 ff.: tale of Kunuk).

140 Boas (1888).

141 See p. 59.

142 See nn. 17, 18, 93 and 94 in this chapter. See, in particular, Wrangell (1839, p. 132), also Porter (1893, pp. 138, 141).

143 Boas (1888, p. 605; 1901, p. 184).

144 See p. 75.

145 The comparison has been made by Weber in Porter (1893, p. 106) and Wells and Kelly (1890, p. 28).

146 Nelson (1899, pp. 303 ff.).
147 Nelson (1899, p. 305); see also Jacobsen (1884, p. 281).
148 Hall (1864, vol. 2, p. 320) states: 'The exchange of gifts is intended to produce an abundance of riches.' This perhaps explains things better than the entire potlatch hypothesis.
149 See chapter 2 nn. 16 and 17. All writers agree that each family is absolutely independent.
150 See chapter 2 nn. 16-22.
151 See chapter 2 nn. 33-40. On relations within the family, see Parry (1824, p. 534) and Lyon (1824, p. 351).
152 To the contrary, see Cranz (1765, III, 3, 25), who says that the Eskimo always enter the winter house at one and the same time.
153 On adoption in general, see Steinmetz (1893), who notes Eskimo data.
154 Lyon (1824, p. 303) and Lewis (1904, p. 55). It is evident from Hanserâk's lists given in Holm (1888, p. 183) that most families have taken in at least one or two strangers.
155 For Greenland, Rink (1875, tale no. 7 on pp. 124 ff.), Holm (1888, tale no. 4, etc.) and Rasmussen (1905, p. 226); for Labrador, Turner (1894, p. 265); for the central Eskimo, Boas (1888, pp. 602 ff.; 1901, pp. 309 ff.) and Petitot (1886, p. 8); for Alaska, Nelson (1899, p. 510 ff.).
156 The absence of a *provider* has a considerable effect on the life of old people who can claim food from their children as long as they can follow them.
157 See nn. 45 and 46 in this chapter. Cranz (1765, III, 4, 28) seems to indicate that it is indeed this phenomenon that, in Greenland, resulted in adoption.
158 Examples in Hall (1864, vol. 2, pp. 214, 219).
159 Dalager (1758, p. 96), H. P. Egede (1741, p. 88), Cranz (1765, III, 3, 25; III, 4, 41), Lyon (1824, p. 349), Hanbury (1904, p. 42, which mentions the offer of women) and Petitot (1887, p. 142).
160 On the permanent exchange of women, see p. 69; on the results of these exchanges, see Schanz in Porter (1893, p. 103).
161 On the eastern, western and central regions, see p. 71 and nn. 112-19; see also Boas (1901, pp. 116, 211, note in a tale).
162 For Greenland, see n. 116 in this chapter.

Chapter 5 Conclusion

1 For examples, see the tale in Boas (1901, p. 335): every night is spent in the *kashim*.
2 The difference stands out in Carstensen (1890, p. 127).
3 Rink (1875, p. 80). The increase in the number of houses is considered by Ryberg as progress toward a European way of life. See chapter 1, Table 1, note c.
4 See, in general, Niblack (1890).
5 See Mauss (1906, pp. 202-4).

6 Boas (1897) and Durkheim (1900a, p. 336).

7 Boas (1897, p. 418). [Boas actually writes as follows: 'The Indians express this alternating of seasons by saying that in summer the *bā'xus* is on top, the *ts'ets'aēga* below, and vice versa in the winter.' Earlier in the same paragraph, Boas explains that *bā'xus* refers to those who have not been initiated and might be translated as 'profane'. *Ts'ets'aēga*, the secrets, designates the winter ceremony itself. JJF.]

8 Mindeleff (1898); see also Durkheim (1904b, p. 663).

9 For a study of Wallachian seasonal migrations, see de Martonne (1902, p. 107).

10 Davids and Oldenberg (1881, pp. 298 ff.). See Oldenberg (1903, p. 360), Kern (1901-3, vol. 2, pp. 5, 42; 1896, p. 42).

11 See the tale in Rink (1875, p. 189) in which a woman is happy to leave the settlement and complains of having had too many visitors. Note Jacobsen's happiness at escaping from the constant frenzied activity of a winter house (1884, p. 241).

12 Woolfe in Porter (1893, p. 137) on the tribe at Icy Cape and Point Kay; Murdoch (1892, p. 80) on the camp of Imekpun in 1883.

13 See some information along these lines in Durkheim (1897, pp. 100-2).

14 Regarding the idea of time, Hubert (1905) has recently arrived at a hypothesis about the rhythm of collective life which would explain the formation of the calendar.

15 See Durkheim (1904a, pp. 137 ff.).

16 See Durkheim (1902).

17 See Durkheim (1897, chapters 2-4).

18 Durkheim and Mauss (1903).

19 The editing and correcting of proofs for this work were mainly done by Marcel Mauss. Henri Beuchat is not responsible for any errors.

Bibliography

anonymous (1904) 'The Eskimo exodus', *Geographical Journal*, 23, 392.

Anderson, James (1856) 'Letter from Chief-Factor James Anderson, to Sir George Simpson . . . Governor in Chief of Rupert Land', *Journal of the Royal Geographical Society*, 26, 18-25.

Anderson, James (1857) 'Extracts from the Chief-Factor James Anderson's Arctic journal', *Journal of the Royal Geographical Society*, 27, 321-8.

Andersson, Gunnar (1902) 'Zur Pflanzengeographie der Arktis', *Geographische Zeitschrift*, 8, 1-22.

L'Année sociologique, vols 1-9, 1898-1906, Paris, Alcan.

Arctic Pilot, 1898-1905, British Admiralty, Hydrographic Office, London.

Armstrong, Alexander (1857) *A Personal Narrative of the Discovery of the North West Passage*, London, Hurst & Blackett.

Astrup, Eivind (1898) *With Peary near the Pole*, London, C. A. Pearson.

Back, George (1836) *Narrative of the Arctic Land Expedition to the Mouth of the Great Fish River and along the Shores of the Arctic Ocean, in the Years 1833, 1834 and 1835*, London, John Murray.

Bahnson, Kristian (1892) *Etnografien fremstillet i dens Hovedtraek*, Copenhagen, Nordiske Førlag, vol. 1.

Ballantyne, R. M. (1867) *Ungava: a Tale of Esquimaux Land*, London, Nelson.

Barrow, John (Sir) (1846) *Voyages of Discovery and Research within the Arctic Regions* . . ., London, John Murray.

Bartholomew, J. G. (1899) *Atlas of Meteorology: a Series of over Four Hundred Maps*, prepared by J. G. Bartholomew and A. J. Herbertson, and edited by Alex Buchan . . . Under the patronage of the Royal Geographical Society, prepared by the Edinburgh Geographical Institute, Westminster, A. Constable.

Beechey, F. W. (1831) *Narrative of a Voyage to the Pacific and Beering's Strait*, 2 vols, London, Henry Colburn & Richard Bentley.

Bellot, J. R. (1854) *Journal d'un voyage aux Mers Polaires, exécuté à la recherche de Sir John Franklin, en 1851 et 1852* . . ., Paris, Perrotin.

Berghaus, H. (1850–2) 'Physikalischer Atlas', *Geographisches Jahrbuch zur Mittheilung aller wichtigern neuen Erforschungen von H. Berghaus*, nos 1–4, Gotha.

Bessels, Emil (1879) *Die amerikanische Nordpol-Expedition*, Leipzig, W. Engelmann.

Bessels, Emil (1884) 'The northernmost inhabitants of the earth: an ethnographic sketch', *American Naturalist*, 18, 861–82.

Boas, Franz (1883) 'Über die ehemalige Verbreitung der Eskimos im arktisch-amerikanischen Archipel', *Zeitschrift der Gesellschaft für Erdkunde*, 18, 118–36.

Boas, Franz (1888) 'The Central Eskimos', *Sixth Annual Report of the Bureau of American Ethnology*, 399–669.

Boas, Franz (1891) 'The Indians of British Columbia: Lku'ñgen, Nootka, Kwakiutl, Shuswap', in Sixth Report on the North-Western Tribes of Canada, 1890, *Report of the British Association for the Advancement of Science*, 553–715.

Boas, Franz (1897) 'The social organization and the secret societies of the Kwakiutl Indians', *Annual Report of the U.S. National Museum for 1895*, 311–738.

Boas, Franz (1899) 'Property marks of the Alaskan Eskimo', *American Anthropologist*, n.s. 1, 601–13.

Boas, Franz (1901) 'The Eskimo of Baffin Land and Hudson Bay', *Bulletin of the American Museum of Natural History*, 15, 1–570.

Boas, Franz (1904) 'The folk-lore of the Eskimo', *Journal of American Folklore*, 17, 1–13.

Boas, Franz and Rink, H. J. (1889) 'Eskimo tales and songs', *Journal of American Folklore*, 2, 123–31.

Bouglé, C. (1903) 'Revue générale des théories récentes sur la division du travail', *L'Année sociologique*, 6, 73–122.

Canada, Geological Survey, *Report*, 1898, Ottawa.

Carstensen, A. C. R. (1890) *Two Summers in Greenland: an Artist's Adventures among Ice and Islands, in Fiords and Mountains*, London, Chapman & Hall.

Cartwright, George (1792) *A Journal of Transactions and Events during a Residence of nearly Sixteen Years on the Coast of Labrador* . . ., 3 vols, London, Newark, Allin & Ridge.

Chappell, Edward (1817) *Narrative of a Voyage to Hudson's Bay in his Majesty's Ship 'Rosamond', Comprising some Account of the North-Eastern Coast of America, etc.*, London, J. Mawman.

Coats, William (1852) *The Geography of Hudson's Bay: Being the Remarks of Captain W. Coats, in Many Voyages to that Locality, between the Years 1727 and 1751*, ed. J. Barrow, London, Hakluyt Society (reprint, New York, Burt Franklin, n.d.).

Cranz, David (1765) *Historie von Grönland, enthaltend die Beschreibung des Landes und der Einwohner, insbesondere die Geschichte der dortigen Mission der Evangelischen Brüder zu Neu-Herrnhut und Lichtenfels*, 2 vols, Leipzig, Barby.

Cranz, David (1767) *The History of Greenland*, 2 vols, London, Longman, Hurst, Rees, Orme & Brown.

Cranz, David (1770) *Fortsetzung der Historie von Grönland . . . von 1763 bis 1768, nebst beträchtlichen Zusätzen und Anmerkungen zur natürlichen Geschichte*, Leipzig, Barby.

Dalager, Lars (1758) *Grønlandske Relationer*, ed. L. Bobé, Copenhagen (reprinted in 1915 in *Grønlandske Selskab*, Skrifter 2).

Dall, W. H. (1870) *Alaska and its Resources*, Boston, Lee & Shepard, vol. 1.

Dall, W. H. (1877) 'Tribes of the extreme north-west', *Contributions to North American Ethnology*, 1, 1-156.

Davids, T. W. Rhys and Oldenberg, Hermann (trans.) (1881) 'Vinaya Texts', pt I in *Sacred Books of the East*, 13, 71-355, Oxford University Press (reprint, Delhi, Motilal Banarsidass, 1965).

Davis, John (1589) 'The first voyage of Master John Davis, undertaken in June 1585: for the discoverie of the Northwest Passage. Written by John James Marchant, Servant to the worshipfull M. William Sanderson', in Hakluyt, 1589, 776-80.

Davis, W. M. (1903) 'A scheme of geography', *Geographical Journal*, 22, 413-23.

Dease, P. W. and Simpson, Thomas (1838) 'An account of the recent Arctic discoveries of Messrs. Dease and T. Simpson', *Journal of the Royal Geographical Society*, 8, 213-25.

Dease, P. W. and Simpson, Thomas (1839) 'An account of Arctic discovery on the northern shore of America in the summer of 1838', *Journal of the Royal Geographical Society*, 9, 325-30.

Demangeon, Albert (1905) *La Plaine Picarde: Picardie-Arlois-Cambrésis-Beauvaisis: Étude de géographie sur les plaines de craie du Nord de la France . . .*, Paris, A. Colin.

Dobbs, Arthur (1744) *An Account of the Countries Adjoining to Hudson's Bay (in the North-west Part of America . . .)*, London, J. Robinson.

Drygalski, Erich von (1897) *Grönland-Expedition der Gesellschaft für Erdkunde zu Berlin, 1891-1893, unter Leitung von Erich von Drygalski*, 2 vols, Berlin, Gesellschaft für Erdkunde.

Durkheim, Émile (1897) *Le Suicide; étude de sociologie*, Paris, Alcan (*Suicide: a Study in Sociology*, trans. J. A. Spaulding and G. Simpson, London, Routledge & Kegan Paul, 1952).

Durkheim, Émile (1899a) 'Morphologie sociale', *L'Année sociologique*, 2, 520-1.

Durkheim, Émile (1899b) Review of Ratzel, *Politische Geographie, L'Année sociologique*, 2, 522-32.

Durkheim, Émile (1900a) Review of Boas, 'The social organization and the secret societies of the Kwakiutl Indians', *L'Année sociologique*, 3, 336-40.

Durkheim, Émile (1900b) Review of Ratzel, *Anthropogeographie*, vol. 1, *L'Année sociologique*, 3, 550-8.

Durkheim, Émile (1901) Review of Ratzel, *Das Meer als Quelle der Volkergrösse* and 'Der Ursprung und die Wanderungen der Völker geographisch betrachtet', *L'Année sociologique*, 4, 565-8.

Durkheim, Émile (1902) *De la Division du travail social*, 2nd ed., Paris, Alcan (*The Division of Labour in Society*, Free Press, 1947).

Durkheim, Émile (1903) Review of Schrader, 'Le Facteur planétaire de l'évolution humaine' and 'Lois terrestres et coutumes humaines', *L'Année sociologique*, 6, 539–40.

Durkheim, Émile (1904a) *Les Règles de la méthode sociologique*, 3rd ed., Paris, Alcan.

Durkheim, Émile (1904b) Review of Mindeleff, 'Navaho houses', *L'Année sociologique*, 7, 663.

Durkheim, Émile and Mauss, Marcel (1903) 'De quelques formes primitives de classification; contribution à l'étude des représentations collectives', *L'Année sociologique*, 6, 1–72 (*Primitive Classification*, trans. R. Needham, London, Cohen & West, and University of Chicago Press, 1963).

Egede, Hans Povelson (1741) *Det gamle Grønlands nye Perlustration, eller Naturelhistorie, og Beskrivelse over det gamle Grønlands Situation, Luft, Temperament og Beskaffenhed 1721-1736*, Copenhagen (enlarged edition of a work first published in 1729, trans. and published in English in 1745, in French in 1763; reprinted in *Meddelelser om Grønland*, 54 (1925)).

Egede, H. P. (1745) *A Description of Greenland, Shewing the Natural History, Situation, Boundaries and Face of the Country*, London, C. Hitch.

Egede, H. P. (1763) *Description et histoire naturelle du Groenland*, trans. Des Roches de Parthenay, Copenhagen and Geneva, C. & A. Philibert.

Egede, Poul Hansen (1741) *Continuation af Relationerne betreffende den Grønlandske Missions Tilstand og Beskaffenhed* (forfattet i form af en journal fra anno 1734 till 1740, etc.), ed. Hans Egede, Copenhagen.

Egede, P. H. (1750) *Dictionarium Grönlandico-Danico-Latinum*, Copenhagen.

Egede, P. H. (1788) *Efterretninger om Grønland* (uddragne af en journal holden fra 1721 till 1788), Copenhagen.

Elliott, H. W. (1886) *Our Arctic Province: Alaska and the Seal Islands*, New York, Scribner.

Ellis, Henry (1748) *A Voyage to Hudson's Bay . . . in . . . 1746 and 1747, for Discovering a North West Passage . . .*, London, H. Whitridge.

Erdmann, Friedrich (1864) *Eskimoisches Wörterbuch gesammelt von den Missionaren in Labrador*, Baudissin, E. H. Monse.

Faustini, A. (1903) 'L'esodo Eskimese: un capitolo di anthropogeografia artica', *Rivista di Fisica*, Pavia, 4, 28.

Fewkes, J. W. (1896) 'The Tusayan ritual: a study of the influence of environment on Aboriginal cults', *Annual Report of the Board of Regents of the Smithsonian Institution to July 1895*, 625-37.

Fox, Luke (1635) *North-West Fox; or Fox from the North-West Passage . . . Together with . . . Mr. James Hall's Three Voyages to Greynland*, London, Alsop & Fawcet.

Franklin, John (Sir) (1823) *Narrative of a Journey to the Shores of the Polar Sea, in the Years 1819-20-21-22*, London, John Murray.

Franklin, John (1828) *Narrative of a Second Expedition to the Shores of the Polar Sea, in the Years 1825, 1826 and 1827*, London, John Murray.

Frobisher, Martin (1867) *The Three Voyages of Martin Frobisher*, ed. R. Collinson, Hakluyt Society, vol. 38, London (reprint, New York, Burt Franklin, n.d.).

Gilder, W. H. (1881) *Schwatka's Search, Sledging in the Arctic in Quest of the Franklin Records*, New York, Scribner.

Graah, W. A. (1832) *Undersøgelses-Reise til Østkysten af Grønland . . . 1828-1831*, Copenhagen (new ed. by Kaj Birket-Smith, Copenhagen, Gyldendal-Nordisk Førlag, 1932).

Greely, A. W. (1886) *Three Years of Arctic Service: an Account of the Lady Franklin Bay Expedition of 1881-1884 and the Attainment of the Farthest North*, 2 vols, London, R. Bentley, and New York, Scribner.

Hakluyt, Richard (1589) *The Principall Navigations, Voiages and Discoveries of the English Nation*, London, Bishop & Newberie.

Hall, C. F. (1864) *Life with the Esquimaux*, 2 vols, London, Sampson Low, Son & Marston.

Hall, C. F. (1879) *Narrative of the Second Arctic Expedition . . .*, ed. J. E. Nourse, Washington, U.S. Government Printing Office.

Hanbury, D. T. (1904) *Sport and Travel in the Northland of Canada*, London, E. Arnold.

Hansen, Johannes (1888) 'Liste over Beboerne af Grønlands Østkyst', *Meddelelser om Grønland*, 10, 183-206.

Hassert, Curt (1895) 'Die Völkerwanderung der Eskimo', *Geographische Zeitschrift*, 1, 302-22.

Hassert, Curt (1902) *Die Polarforschung*, Leipzig, B. G. Teubner.

Hayes, I. I. (1860) *An Arctic Boat Journey in the Autumn of 1854*, ed. N. Shaw, London, R. Bentley.

Hayes, I. I. (1867) *The Open Polar Sea: a Narrative of a Voyage of Discovery Towards the North Pole, in the Schooner 'United States'*, New York, Hurd & Houghton.

Hearne, Samuel (1795) *A Journey from Prince of Wales's Fort in Hudson's Bay to the Northern Ocean . . . in the Years 1769-1772*, London, A. Strahan & T. Cadell.

Hoffman, W. J. (1897) 'The graphic art of the Eskimos', *Annual Report of the U.S. National Museum for 1895*, 739-968.

Holm, G. F. (1887-8) 'Østgrønlandske Expedition, 1883-1885, Beretninger', published in various parts in *Meddelelser om Grønland*, 9-10.

Holm, G. F. (1888) 'Ethnologisk Skizze av Angmagsalikerne (Østgrønlandske Expedition, 1883-1885)', *Meddelelser om Grønland*, 10, 43-182 (trans. and published in English as 'Ethnological sketch of the Angmagsalik Eskimo', *Meddelelser om Grønland*, 39, 1-147: includes 'Sagn og Fortaellinger').

Holm, G. F. (1894) 'Oprettelsen af Missions og Handelsstationen Angmagsalik paa Grønlands Østkyst', *Geografisk Tidsskrift*, 12, 247-55.

Holm, G. F. (1895) 'Is og Vejrforholdene', *Geografisk Tidsskrift*, 13.

Hooper, W. H. (1853) *Ten Months among the Tents of the Tuski, with*

Incidents of an Arctic Boat Expedition in Search of Sir John Franklin, London, John Murray.

Hubbard, G. G. (1896) 'The Japanese nation: a typical product of environment', *Annual Report of the Board of Regents of the Smithsonian Institution to July 1895*, 667-81.

Hubert, Henri (1905) 'Étude sommaire de la représentation du temps dans la religion et la magie', *Rapport de l'École Pratique des Hautes Études: Section des sciences religieuses*, Paris, Imprimerie Nationale.

Isachsen, G. (1903) 'Die Wanderungen der östlichen Eskimo nach und in Grönland', *Petermanns geographische Mitteilungen*, 49, 150-1.

Jacobsen, J. A. (1884) *Captain Jacobsen's Reise an der Nordwestküste Amerikas, 1881-1883*, ed. A. Woldt, Leipzig, M. Spohr (*Alaskan Voyage*, trans. E. Gunther, University of Chicago Press, 1977).

Kane, E. K. (1856) *Arctic Explorations: the Second Grinnell Expedition in Search of Sir J. Franklin, 1853, '54, '55*, 2 vols, Philadelphia, Childs & Peterson.

Kern, J. H. C. (1896) *Manual of Indian Buddhism*, Strassburg, K. J. Trübner.

Kern, J. H. C. (1901-3) *Histoire de Bouddhisme dans L'Inde*, 2 vols, Paris, E. Leroux.

Kleinschmidt, S. P. (1871) *Den Grønlandske Ordbog*, Copenhagen, L. Klein.

Klutschak, H. W. (1881a) *Als Eskimo unter den Eskimos*, Vienna, Pest, Leipzig, Hartleben.

Klutschak, H. W. (1881b) 'Die Eskimos von Hudson-Bai', *Deutsche Rundschau für Geographie und Statistik*, 3, 417-23.

Kornerup, A. N. (1880) 'Bemaerkninger om Grønlands almindelige Naturforhold', *Meddelelser om Grønland*, 3, xxvii-xxxvi, 224-31.

Krause, Aurel and Krause, Arthur (1882) 'Die Expedition der Bremer geographischen Gesellschaft nach der Tschuktschen-Halbinsel und Alaska 1881-1882 (Reisebriefe der Gebrüder Krause)', *Deutsche geographische Blätter*, 5, 1-35; 111-53; 177-223.

Kroeber, A. L. (1899) 'The Eskimo of Smith Sound', *Bulletin of the American Museum of Natural History*, 12, 265-327.

Kumlien, Ludwig (1879) 'Contributions to the natural history of Arctic America, made in connection with the Howgate Polar Expedition, 1877-1878', *Bulletin of the U.S. National Museum*, 15, 1-179.

Lewis, Arthur (1904) *The Life and Work of the Rev. E. J. Peck among the Eskimos, etc.*, London, Hodder & Stoughton.

Lyon, G. F. (1824) *The Private Journal of Captain G. F. Lyon, of H.M.S. 'Hecla', during the Recent Voyage of Discovery under Captain Parry*, London, John Murray.

Lyon, G. F. (1825) *A Brief Narrative of an Unsuccessful Attempt to Reach Repulse Bay, through Sir Thomas Rowe's 'Welcome', in His Majesty's Ship 'Griper' in the Year 1824*, London, John Murray.

MacClure, R. J. Le Mesurier (Sir) (1853) *The North-West Passage: Capt. MacClure's Despatches from Her Majesty's Discovery Ship, 'Investigator' off Point Warren and Cape Bathurst*, London, J. Betts.

McGee, W. J. (1896) 'The Relation of Institutions to Environment',

Annual Report of the Board of Regents of the Smithsonian Institution to July 1895, 701-11.

Mackinder, H. J. (1904) 'The geographical pivot of history', *Geographical Journal*, 23, 421-44.

Maclean, John (1849) *Notes of a Twenty-Five Years' Service in the Hudson's Bay Territory*, 2 vols, London, Bentley.

Markham, A. H. (Sir) (1874) *A Whaling Cruise to Baffin's Bay and the Gulf of Boothia, and an Account of the Rescue of the Crew of the 'Polaris'*, London, S. Low, Marston, Low & Searle.

Markham, A. H. (1878) *The Great Frozen Sea; a Personal Narrative of the Voyage of the 'Alert' during the Arctic Expedition of 1875-1876*, London, Daldy & Isbister.

Markham, C. R. (Sir) (1875) 'Papers on the Greenland Eskimos', Royal Geographical Society, *Arctic Geography and Ethnology*, 163-229.

Martonne, Emmanuel de (1897) 'La vie des peuples du Haut-Nil', *Annales de Géographie*, 1896, 506-21.

Martonne, E. de (1902) *La Valachie: essai de monographie géographique*, Paris, A. Colin.

Mason, O. T. (1896a) 'Primitive travel and transportation', *Annual Report of the U.S. National Museum for 1894*, 239-617.

Mason, O. T. (1896b) 'Influence of environment upon human industries or arts', *Annual Report of the Board of Regents of the Smithsonian Institution to July 1895*, 639-65.

Mauss, Marcel (1905) Review of Boas, 'The folk-lore of the Eskimo', *L'Année sociologique*, 8, 349.

Mauss, M. (1906) Review of Goddard, 'Life and culture of the Hupa', *L'Année sociologique*, 9, 202-4.

Miertsching, J. A. (1864) *Reisetagebuch bei der Nordpol-Expedition auf dem Schiff 'Investigator'*, 3rd ed., Leipzig, H. Schultze.

Mindeleff, Cosmos (1898) 'Navaho houses', *Seventeenth Annual Report of the Bureau of American Ethnology*, pt 2, 469-517.

The Moravians in Labrador, 1833, Edinburgh, W. Whyte.

Morgan, L. H. (1871) 'Systems of consanguinity and affinity of the human family', *Smithsonian Contributions to Knowledge*, 17, 291-382.

Murdoch, John (1885) 'A study of the Eskimo bows in the U.S. National Museum', *Annual Report of the U.S. National Museum for 1884*, pt 2, 307-16.

Murdoch, John (1892) 'Ethnological results of the Point Barrow expedition', *Ninth Annual Report of the Bureau of American Ethnology*, 1-441.

Nansen, Fridtjof (1903) *Eskimoleben*, trans. from Norwegian by M. Langfeldt, Leipzig, Meyer.

Nelson, E. W. (1899) 'The Eskimo about Bering Strait', *Eighteenth Annual Report of the Bureau of American Ethnology*, pt 1, 3-518.

Niblack, Albert (1890) 'The Coast Indians of Southern Alaska and Northern British Columbia', *Annual Report of the U.S. National Museum for 1888*, 225-386.

Nordenskiöld, N. A. E. (1880-1) *Vega's färd kring Asien och Europa*, 2 vols, Stockholm, F. & G. Beijer.

Nordenskiöld, N. A. E. (1881) *The Voyage of the 'Vega' round Asia and Europe*, trans. A. Leslie, 2 vols, London, Macmillan.

Nordenskiöld, N. A. E. (1883) *Voyage de la 'Vega' autour de l'Asie et de l'Europe*, trans. from Swedish by C. Rabot and C. Lallemand, 2 vols, Paris, Hachette.

Nordenskiöld, N. A. E. (1885) *Den andra Dicksonska Expeditionen till Grönland dess inre isöken och dess ostkust utförd år 1883 befäl af* (and now described by) A. E. Nordenskiöld, Stockholm, F. & G. Beijer.

Oldenberg, Hermann (1903) *Le Bouddha, sa vie, sa doctrine, sa communauté*, trans. from German by A. Foucher, Paris, Alcan.

Packard, A. S. (the younger) (1891) *The Labrador Coast: a Journal of Two Summer Cruises*, New York, N. D. C. Hodges.

Parry, W. E. (1821), *Journal of a Voyage for the Discovery of a North-West Passage from the Atlantic to the Pacific; Performed in the Years 1819-20, in His Majesty's Ships 'Hecla' and 'Griper' under the Orders of William Edward Parry*, London, John Murray.

Parry, W. E. (1824) *Journal of a Second Voyage for the Discovery of a North-West Passage from the Atlantic to the Pacific; Performed in the Years 1821-22-23, in His Majesty's Ships 'Fury' and 'Hecla', under the Orders of Captain William Edward Parry*, London, John Murray.

Parry, W. E. (1825) *Appendix to Captain Parry's Journal of a Second Voyage for the Discovery of a North-West Passage from the Atlantic to the Pacific, Performed in His Majesty's Ships 'Fury' and 'Hecla', in the Years 1821-22-23*, London, John Murray.

Peary, J. D. (1893) *My Arctic Journal: a Year among Ice Fields and Eskimos . . . With an Account of the Great White Journey across Greenland by R. E. Peary*, New York, Contemporary Pub. Co., and London, Longmans.

[Peary, J. D.] (1903) *Children of the Arctic*, by the Snow Baby and her Mother [Josephine D. Peary], London, Isbister.

Peary, R. E. (1898) *Northward over the 'Great Ice'*, 2 vols, New York and London, Methuen.

Periodical Accounts Relating to the Missions of the Church of the United Brethren, Established among the Heathen, 1790-1889, 34 vols, London.

Petitot, E. F. S. (1876) *Monographie des Esquimaux Tchiglit*, Paris, E. Leroux.

Petitot, E. F. S. (1886) 'Traditions indiennes du Canada nord-ouest', in *Les Littératures populaires de toutes les nations*, 23, Paris, Maisonneuve frères & Ch. Leclerc.

Petitot, E. F. S. (1887) *Les grands Esquimaux*, Paris, Plon.

Petroff, Ivan (1884) 'Report on the population, industries, and resources of Alaska', *Tenth Census of the United States*, Washington, Government Printing Office.

Pilling, J. C. (1887) *Bibliography of the Eskimo Language*, Washington, Government Printing Office.

Pinart, A. L. (1873) 'Esquimaux et Koloches: idées religieuses et traditions des Kaniagmiouks', *Revue d'Anthropologie*, 2, 673-80.

Porter, R. P. (1893) *Report on the Population and Resources of Alaska at the 11th Census, 1890*, Washington.

Powell, J. W. (1896) 'Relation of primitive peoples to environment', *Annual Report of the Board of Regents of the Smithsonian Institution to July 1895*, 625-37.

Preuss, K. Th. (1899) 'Die ethnographische Veränderung der Eskimos des Smithsundes', *Ethnologisches Notizblatt, Königliches Museum für Völkerkunde*, Berlin, 2, i, 38-43.

Ramsay, W. M. (1902) 'The geographical conditions determining history and religion in Asia Minor', *Geographical Journal*, 20, 257-82.

Rasmussen, K. J. V. (1905) *Nye Mennesker*, Copenhagen and Kristiania, Gyldendal-Nordisk forlag.

Ratzel, Friedrich (1891) *Anthropogeographie*, vol. 2, Stuttgart, J. Engelhorn.

Ratzel, F. (1895) 'Studien über politische Räume', *Geographische Zeitschrift*, 1, 163-82.

Ratzel, F. (1897) *Politische Geographie*, Munich and Leipzig, R. Oldenbourg.

Ratzel, F. (1899) *Anthropogeographie*, vol. 1, 2nd ed., Stuttgart, J. Engelhorn.

Ratzel, F. (1900) 'Le sol, la société et l'état', *L'Année sociologique*, 3, 1-14.

Ratzel, F. (1903) *Politische Geographie, oder die Geographie der Staaten, des Verkehres und des Krieges*, 2nd rev. ed., Munich and Berlin.

Richardson, John (Sir) (1851) *Arctic Searching Expedition: a Journal of a Boat-Voyage through Rupert's Land and the Arctic Sea, in Search of the Discovery Ships under Command of Sir John Franklin*, 2 vols, London, Longman, Brown, Green & Longmans.

Richardson, John (1861) *The Polar Regions*, Edinburgh, A. & C. Black.

Riedel, F. (1902) 'Die Polarvölker: Eine durch naturbedingte Züge charakterisierte Völkergruppe', inaugural dissertation, Halle.

Rikli, Martin (1903) *Die Pflanzenwelt des hohen Norden*, St Gallen.

Rink, H. J. (1857) *Grønland, geografisk og statistisk beskrevet*, 2 vols, Copenhagen, L. Klein.

Rink, H. J. (1860) *Kaladlit assilialiat*, pts I-IV, Godthaab (Eskimo edition of *Tales and Traditions of the Eskimo*).

Rink, H. J. (1866-71) *Eskimoiske Eventyr og Sagn*, 2 vols, Copenhagen, C. A. Reitzel.

Rink, H. J. (1875) *Tales and Traditions of the Eskimo, with a Sketch of their Habits, Religion, Language and other Peculiarities*, ed. R. Brown, Edinburgh and London, W. Blackwood.

Rink, H. J. (1877) *Danish Greenland: its People and its Products*, ed. R. Brown, London, H. S. King.

Rink, H. J. (1886) 'Østgrønlaenderne i deres Forhold til Vestgrønlaenderne og de øverige Eskimostammer', *Geografisk Tidsskrift*, 8, 139-45.

Rink, H. J. (1887) 'The Eskimo tribes; their distribution and characteristics, especially in regard to language', vol. 1, *Meddelelser om Grønland*, 11, 1-163.

Rink, H. J. (1891) Supplement to 'The Eskimo tribes; their distribution and characteristics, especially in regard to language', *Meddelelser om Grønland*, 11, supplement, 1-124.

Rink, Signe (ed.) (1900) *Vestgrønlaender Kateket Hanseråks Dagbog om de hedenske Østgrønlaendere ført under den 'Danske Konebaads Expeditions' Reise til Grønlands Østkyst*, Copenhagen, Hagerup.

Ross, John (Sir) (1819) *A Voyage of Discovery Made under the Orders of the Admiralty, in H.M.S. 'Isabella' and 'Alexander', for the Purpose of Exploring Baffin's Bay and Inquiring into the Probability of a North-West Passage*, London, John Murray.

Ross, John (1835) *Narrative of a Second Voyage in Search of a North-West Passage, and of a Residence in the Arctic Regions during the Years 1829, 1830, 1831, 1832, 1833* . . ., London, Webster.

Ryberg, Carl (1894) 'Om Erhvervs- og Befolkningsforholdene i Grønland', *Geografisk Tidsskrift*, 12, i, 87-110; ii, 113-31.

Ryberg, Carl (1898) 'Fra Missions og Handelsstationen ved Angmagssalik', *Geografisk Tidsskrift*, 14, 116-23, 169-72.

Ryberg, Carl (1904) 'Om Erhvervs- og Befolkningsforholdene i Grønland samt Bemaerkninger til Oplysning om Grønlaendernes nuvaerende Tilstand', *Geografisk Tidsskrift*, 17, 69-92.

Ryder, C. H. (1895a) 'Beretning om den østgrønlandske Expedition, 1891-1892', *Meddelelser om Grønland*, 17, 1-159.

Ryder, C. H. (1895b) 'Om den tidligere eskimoiske Bebyggelse af Scoresby Sund, *Meddelelser om Grønland*, 17, 281-343.

Schultz, J. C. (1895) 'The Innuits of our Arctic Coast', *Royal Society of Canada, Transactions*, 1894, vol. 12, section 2, 113-34.

Schultz-Lorentzen, C. W. (1904) 'Eskimoernes Indvandring i Grønland', *Meddelelser om Grønland*, 26, 289-330.

Schwatka, Frederick (1884) 'The Netschilluk Innuits', *Science*, 4, 543-5.

Schwatka, F. (1885) *Nimrod in the North: or Hunting and Fishing Adventures in the Arctic Regions*, New York, Cassell.

Simpson, John (1875) 'The western Eskimo: observations on the western Eskimo and the country they inhabit', Royal Geographical Society, *Arctic Geography and Ethnology*, 233-75.

Simpson, Thomas (1843) *Narrative of the Discoveries on the North Coast of America, Effected by the Officers of the Hudson Bay Company 1836-1839*, London, R. Bentley.

Stearns, W. A. (1884) *Labrador: a Sketch of its Peoples, its Industries, and its Natural History*, Boston, Lee & Shepard.

Steensby, H. P. (1905) *Om Eskimo Kulturens Oprindelse, en etnografisk og antropogeografisk Studie*, Copenhagen, Salmonsen.

Steinmetz, S. R. (1894) *Ethnologische Studien zur ersten Entwicklung der Strafe*, vol. 1, Leiden, S. C. van Doesburgh, and Leipzig, O. Harrassowitz.

Steinmetz, S. R. (1892) vol. 2, dissertation, Leiden, S. C. van Doesburgh.

Steinmetz, S. R. (1893) 'De "Fosterage" of opvoeding in vreemde families', *Tijdschrift van het Koninklijk Nederlandsch Aardrijkskundig Genootschap*, 10, 477-529, 903-21, 1092-1111.

Sverdrup, O. N. (1903) *Nyt land; fire Aar i arktiske Egne*, 2 vols, Kristiania, H. Aschehoug.

Sverdrup, O. N. (1904) *New Land; Four Years in the Arctic Regions*, trans. E. H. Hearn, 2 vols, London and New York, Longmans.

Thalbitzer, William (1904) 'A phonetical study of the Eskimo language', *Meddelelser om Grønland*, 31, 1-406.

Turner, L. M. (1894) 'Ethnology of the Ungava District, Hudson Bay Territory', *Eleventh Annual Report of the Bureau of American Ethnology*, 159-350.

Tylor, E. B. (1883-4) 'Old Scandinavian civilization among the modern Esquimaux', *Journal of the Royal Anthropological Institute of Great Britain and Ireland*, 13, 348-57.

Tyrrell, J. W. (1898) *Across the Sub-Arctics of Canada: a Journey of 3200 Miles by Canoe and Snowshoe through the Barren Lands*, London, T. F. Unwin.

U.S. Coast and Geodetic Survey, 1901, *Bulletin* 40, Alaska.

Vacher, A. (1905) Review of Vidal de la Blache, *Tableau de la géographie de la France*, *L'Année sociologique*, 8, 613-15.

Vidal de la Blache, Paul (1903a) 'La géographie humaine, ses rapports avec la géographie de la vie', *Revue de Synthèse Historique*, 3, 219-40.

Vidal de la Blache, P. (1903b) *Tableau de la géographie de la France*, Paris, Hachette.

Wächter, Ernst (1898) 'Die grönländischen Eskimo', *Die Natur*, 47, 37-40.

Warming, Eugenius (1888) 'Om Naturen i det nordligste Grønland', *Geografisk Tidsskrift*, 9, 131-46.

Wells, Roger and Kelly, J. W. (1890) 'English-Eskimo and Eskimo-English vocabularies', *U.S. Bureau of Education, Circular of Information*, ii, 1-72.

Wrangell, F. P. (1839) 'Statistische und ethnographische Nachrichten über die russischen Besitzungen an der Nordwestküste von Amerika', *Beiträge zur Kenntnis des russischen Reiches und der angrenzenden Länder*, St Petersburg, vol. 1, 1-332.

Index

The letter f after a page number indicates a figure or map.